MW01599048

Excellent Online Science Teaching: Effective Strategies for a Successful Semester

Frances Karels

First Edition

To order, contact:

The Part-Time Press

P.O. Box 130117

Ann Arbor, MI 48113-0117

Phone/Fax: 734-930-6854

First printing: September, 2019

© 2019 The Part-Time Press

ISBN: 978-0-940017-45-0 (paperback)

Printed in the United States of America

Praise for *Excellent Online Science Teaching: Effective Strategies for a Successful Semester*

Excellent Online Science Teaching: Effective Strategies for a Successful Semester, is a fantastic resource for online science faculty—it is applicable to science courses across the natural sciences, including science lab courses and virtual field trip experiences. The book does a superb job of outlining and highlighting tools, strategies, and practices for effective science teaching online, and provides helpful tips and exemplary resources that will benefit any online science educator's toolkit! —*Jill Nugent, Associate Dean, Science, Southern New Hampshire University*

Excellent Online Science Teaching: Effective Strategies for a Successful Semester is a masterfully written guide to creating effective and enjoyable online science courses, and provides a blueprint for the educator new to the format or the professor that needs to brush up on what is available in the world of online learning. From beginning to end, the book...provides practical advice for crafting a course that sets the students up for success. From communication to assessment and everything in between, the reader will be engrossed in the book and it's easy to follow format."—*Amanda Adams, Executive Director for Teaching and Learning, West Independent School District, West, Texas*

Excellent Online Science Teaching is a must-read for anyone preparing to teach science online or has taught science online for years. The author's new ideas and fresh perspective will encourage and inspire readers.—*Andi McNair, Author of Genius Hour: Passion Projects that Ignite Innovation and Student Inquiry* and *A Meaningful Mess: A Teacher's Guide to Student-Driven Classrooms, Authentic Learning, Student Empowerment, and Keeping It All Together without Losing Your Mind*

Table of Contents

Section II: Building the Course

Section III: Facilitating the Course

Table of Figures

Preface

Why Teach Science Online?

Throughout the book, you will learn how online classes can support Adult Learning Principles and fulfill the Principles of Good Practice. I will not specify what content you should teach, but I will recommend best practices in teaching the content, as well as recommending resources you can use in your courses.

You will have your own reasons for teaching online, one of which could be that if you don't start teaching science online now, someone else will and you'll be passed over for course assignments. For me, there were several reasons I wanted to try teaching online. For starters, I love science and trying out innovative technology and teaching strategies. An opportunity to combine them all? Perfect!

I tell my students at the beginning of every semester that I'm a geek, and not ashamed of the fact. Perhaps you feel similarly about technology, and that has led you to online teaching. On the other hand, perhaps you feel you're not that tech savvy. No problem. You've mastered the intricacies of your discipline well enough to teach college, so trust me when I say that you can learn to adopt and adapt technology well enough to use it to teach online. You don't have to know how to build apps or code to teach online, just like you don't have to be a mechanic to be able to drive your car. All you really need is to be open and willing to try innovative technology and instructional strategies.

For students, a primary motivation for choosing online classes is the need for a flexible schedule to accommodate work obligations. In a survey of online learners in 2015, almost two-thirds held full-time jobs (BestColleges.com). Having blended and online classes allows more flexibility of scheduling for students. Thus, with one out of every seven college students enrolled in a fully online program in 2014 (Poulin), can colleges afford to not offer fully online programs?

Online course offerings in higher education have also grown because our students come to college with unique sets of skills, levels of academic preparation, and learning abilities. A broader range of courses and course formats better fits the needs of these diverse student populations.

I began with one blended course (we did everything but labs and exams online), and that course filled up faster than many face-to-face sections of the same course.

On the first day of that blended class, a student asked why that section met less frequently than other sections of the same course. I'd presumed students would see the "Blended/Hybrid Class" label in the course schedule and understand it. Eventually, five or six students dropped that blended science class. Of the students who remained, fewer than 20 percent failed the class, which was comparable to the pass rates in my face-to-face classes. Students told me they'd enjoyed the class, and would like to take more blended or online science courses.

I learned an important lesson from that first blended class. In subsequent semesters, I contacted students before the first day of class via email and explained the differences between blended (or online) classes and face-to-face classes. Oddly, the one consistent student question about my fully online biology course was whether the students would be required to come to campus. As I continued to teach blended and online sections, I discovered several benefits to teaching these types of courses.

I had time to visit my kids' school, make doctor/dentist/vision appointments, and finish those other activities that are difficult to do during the work week. I attended several conventions and community service events. One year, my family wanted to go to Galveston over a long Labor Day weekend. I was able to go with them. I held "office hours" with students online over Wi-Fi. I taught from the beach! Yes!

But, it's not all freedom, travel and teaching from the beach. Teaching science online will be time consuming, just perhaps in different ways than face-to-face classes. For instance, online classes do not have set hours, and students learn at their own pace (within reason) each week. This means they will be working (and sending you questions) on the course while you're out to dinner with your spouse, spending the weekend with your family, or sleeping.

If you have the opportunity, take an online class before you teach an online course. You will learn first hand the online course design and instructor can make a huge difference in the student experience.

Together, we'll review the research. I'll outline strategies and share tips that help students succeed in blended and online courses. You'll read real-life examples of best practices and I'll show you how to implement best practices quickly and effectively. You'll know how to plan, create and facilitate online science courses that are fun to teach and keep students engaged.

The book is divided into three sections: Planning the Course, Building the Course, and Facilitating the Course. These sections are based on the basic course design process educators use in face-to-face courses. In face-to-face courses, we gather our resources and write lesson plans (Plan), and then prepare the lessons for delivery in the classroom (Build), and execute our lesson plans with our students (Facilitate).

I give students tips on how to progress through the course to increase the likelihood of success, and I'll do the same for this book. I have designed this book so that you can read a chapter, think critically about the research and best practices, and complete that portion of the planning or building process.

The third section outlines pedagogical tips, suggestions and strategies to use when teaching students in your course.

Frances Karels

How To Get the Most Out of This Book

An important tool in this book is the use of icons to highlight important information for the reader.

 Keys to Success: Whenever you see this icon, you'll want to take special note. These are tried and true tips, concepts and ideas to help you plan, build and teach your online science courses.

Caution Light: Whenever you see this icon, you'll know what others who have successfully taught science online have discovered NOT to do while planning and teaching their courses.

In addition to the icons, the table of contents is very detailed to get you to the topic that most interests you at the moment. An index has been compiled for ease of use. Finally, at the end of this book, there is a detailed section that deals with copyright guidelines for the college faculty member.

This book is your detailed reference for online teaching and learning. Use this book as a manual, a guide, or for professional reading. It contains practical and informative strategies to assist you. It is written in a user-friendly manner for your convenience. Enjoy it and GOOD TEACHING.

CHAPTER 1
TOOLS FOR THE ONLINE TEACHER

1.1 Personal Technology

During the course design, creation, and facilitation process, you'll work off campus. You'll need technology that allows you to complete your work regardless of your location. I'll discuss what technology I currently have and my reasoning for those choices, and then I'll provide an overview of options for both Mac and PC.

I'll begin with my smartphone since I carry it with me constantly. I used a Samsung Galaxy S8+ smartphone for two years before recently upgrading to a Samsung Galaxy S10. A smartphone with a large screen size makes viewing emails and websites easier. Other instructors choose iPhones. On both types of smartphones, you can access your Learning Management System (LMS) via the Internet just as you would on a laptop or tablet. Some learning management systems even have apps that you can install, but I only access the LMS via my smartphone for urgent situations.

The following wireless providers offer discounts for educators:

- Verizon: Monthly discounts for state government/university employees https://www.verizonwireless.com/discount-program/

- AT&T: Enter your .edu address to check if you're eligible for a discount https://www.att.com/shop/wireless/iru-check-for-discount.html

- T Mobile: Employee discount program. Enter your information to see if you're eligible through your college employer for a discount. https://validate.t-mobile.com/employee-discount

- Sprint: Enter your information to see if you're eligible for a discount through your college employer. https://

businesssolutions.sprint.com/BizIL-Vertical-Discount_
Education.html

Most of the work in building and facilitating classes includes accessing the LMS, recording audio and video, developing course materials, testing online activities and virtual labs, and writing lessons. I find these types of tasks much easier to accomplish on a laptop, so whe I began teaching online, I invested in a high-quality laptop, a Dell XPS laptop with a 250-gig hard drive. I also purchased a 250G external hard drive to use as a backup. (Seven years ago, I lost files because my previous laptop crashed and I had no backup. Lesson learned.)

Before I purchased my new laptop, I asked the advice of the college's technology department. Our school's technology department head recommended I purchase a laptop with the latest generation processor and a large hard drive. I purchased an HP 15.6-inch laptop with 10-hour battery life, 8GB RAM, touchscreen, 7th Generation Intel processor, HD Webcam, and 1TB hard drive. I know; that sounds like a huge hard drive. That's what I thought about my 250GB hard drive on my old laptop, too, until I looked at the drive and realized how many photos, videos, music, audiobooks, eBooks, and screencasts I had accumulated. You never know what you'll need, such as data from your first fully online course.

Backup your files on a regular basis to avoid losing everything if a computer crashes or your USB drive gets lost or broken. You can purchase a 2TB external hard drive for under $100, and USB drives now hold up to 128GB. Backing up to the cloud is also an option for your phone and/or tablet.

The tool I use least for teaching currently is the iPad Air supplied to me by the school district for which I work. That being said, it does have its usefulness due to the extensive battery life and light weight. I use my iPad most when I go to conferences: I take notes on it, check emails, and access the Internet. You can set up email on the iPad through email apps, and access the LMS via the Internet. Sometimes, however, there are compatibility issues with displaying files that were created on a PC. For example, if you use Google Suite or Microsoft Office, formatting may not display correctly on an iOS device, resulting in files not being as easily readable. Also, any website that uses Adobe Flash will not work on an iPad. Because of these issues, and to have a larger screen size, when I'm home or on campus, I use my laptop. If you must choose between purchasing a tablet and laptop, I recommend a laptop. You can purchase a rolling laptop case (I call it my office on wheels) in which you can carry your laptop, lesson plans, student assignments and office supplies.

Multiple laptops and tablets are available that will fill your needs. You'll need a microphone and camera and you'll need enough space on your hard drive in case you cannot access your course files in cloud storage. Extended battery life is crucial. Seek advice from your college's technology department, especially if your course uses specialized course software. To compare prices and features of the latest laptops and tablets available, search for reviews online.

Many colleges have agreements with technology companies so that instructors and students may purchase hardware and software at significantly reduced costs. These programs vary from college to college, and it's possible that adjunct and part-time faculty may be excluded from participating. Through the program at my college, I purchased a year's license to Adobe Creative Cloud and obtained Microsoft Office 365 for free. Your instructional designer or college technology department can tell you what kinds of software are available, their uses and whether you are permitted to purchase discounted hardware/software.

If it turns out you are not permitted to purchase discounted hardware and software through your college, individual computer hardware and software companies offer educator discounts, though those discounts may not be as generous as the ones offered through a college or university purchasing program. Here are just a few of the companies that will offer faculty discounts directly:

- Adobe Education Store – Students and teachers can save 60 percent off Creative Cloud. http://www.adobe.com/creative-cloud/buy/students.html

- Apple Store – College students and instructors are eligible for discount pricing. https://www.apple.com/education/pricelists/

- Texas Instruments – TI allows educators to try equipment for up to two weeks before purchasing. They also offer a Rewards program in which educators can collect points from purchases and redeem them for other purchases. https://education.ti.com/en/customer-support

- thinkEDU – ThinkEDU offers students and educators discounts on computers, software, and accessories. http://thinkedu.com/

- Western Digital Education Store – Students and instructors can save up to 20 percent on purchases, with free shipping. https://www.wdc.com/shop/student-store.html

Since we're discussing smartphones, tablets, and laptops, we can't neglect Internet service. When you consider what smartphone to use, you'll also have a choice in carrier and plan. I have an unlimited data plan, so I don't worry about how much I use each month. By triaging my emails, I can glance at the subject to determine the level of urgency, and I can wait until I have Wi-Fi to respond. Keep in mind that you won't be able to separate emails from your students from other emails from your college. I receive 5-10 emails from McLennan Community College for every one email from a student. If you are like me, and work another job while teaching one or two courses a semester, you'll receive emails from that company/school as well. I receive around 40 emails per day from various campuses in my school district. I log onto my district's WiFi on my smartphone whenever I am at work, and on my home WiFi at home, so most of the time, I am not using cellular data. Ultimately, being logged into WiFi, triaging emails, and accessing the LMS via your smartphone only in urgent situations means that your smartphone data usage for facilitating a class can be kept to a minimum.

The table below shows approximate data usage for Internet activities on a 3G or 4G smartphone. For estimates of total amounts, you can try Verizon's data calculator (https://www.verizonwireless. com/data-calculator/) or another data calculator on the Internet.

Table 1.1A: Sample data use for Internet activities

Activity	Data Use
Email (Text Only)	10KB
Web Access (Internet)	400KB
Streaming Audio	115 MB per hour
One Audio Track Download	7MB
3G Video Streaming	250MB per hour
4G Video Streaming	350MB per hour
Navigation Turn-by-Turn Directions	5MB per hour

(Data Calculator, Verizon Wireless)

If you can travel to your college and use their Internet to upload materials to the LMS, that will lower your home data usage. If not, you can estimate your home Internet usage by accessing a data calculator provided by your Internet Service Provider. Keep this information in mind when assigning students videos to watch, since students in online classes will be using their home Internet just like you will.

1.2 Colleagues, Mentors, and Instructional Designers

The first Principle of Good Practice (Chickering and Gamson) emphasizes communication between students and faculty, but it also applies to instructors new to teaching online. Some of the most valuable resources for developing your online course will be your college's teaching and learning resource center, colleagues, mentors and instructional designers. Seek out colleagues and/or mentors at your college who have been teaching online courses for a while. Your department head should be able to give you some names. You can also go through a few semester course schedules to see names of instructors listed as teaching online courses. Even if these instructors do not teach science, you can ask about the academic preparation of students who enroll in online courses at your college. Ask these colleagues about what they struggled with when they began teaching online and how they improved or overcame specific issues like student procrastination.

To help instructors with using technology for teaching and learning, most colleges offer instructional design assistance (Miller and Stein, 2016). Instructional designers can help save you time and stress, so get to know them. Ask your department head for contact information, or do a search in your college's online website. Instructional designers are usually attached to the Teaching and Learning department, and they help with planning instruction that improves learning and produces desired learning outcomes. The Institute for Learning and Teaching (TILT) at Colorado State University specifically lists assistance with "translating face-to-face classroom courses into online and distance courses" as one of the tasks their instructional designers perform (Chapman and Cantrell). Basically, if you need assistance or have questions about instructional strategies, best practices in teaching, or instructional technology, instructional designers can help.

Depending on the size and type of college, there may be only one instructional designer per campus, or several. At Blinn College, where I began teaching science online in spring 2011, there was only one instructional designer on our campus, and she was often busy. Fortunately, her office was upstairs from mine, so I could just run upstairs, ask my questions, and quickly get back to work. For example, I had a student with an accommodation that allowed him extra time on a quiz, but I didn't know how to set time for an individual student. In less than 5 minutes, my problem was solved, and I even learned how to set up teams for students with similar accommodations to save time later.

 Seek help. You're not the first science instructor to face a particular challenge designing an online course or lab, and the solution will be just a question away.

McLennan Community College has a Center for Teaching and Learning. There, student workers help instructors upload files into the college's LMS, which is a time-saving resource, since uploading files to the LMS can be a tedious process (especially if your course utilizes a lot of video files). The CTL offers a professional development class in teaching online. The CTL is also developing a voluntary online course review system. The system will give me comprehensive feedback on my online courses. Check with your instructional designer to see what your college offers.

What else can an instructional designer do for you and your course? Instructional designers and technologists fill a variety of roles at their colleges, including providing professional development on pedagogy/andragogy and technology, creating online courses, moving courses, or translating face-to-face courses to online delivery, supporting software (including the LMS) used by faculty and students, assisting with accessibility issues, working to minimize cheating, and even producing video or other multimedia (Miller and Stein). Collaboration with an instructional designer can help make your online course well-organized, improve functionality, and ensure accessibility to all students, including those with disabilities.

If you do not have access to an instructional designer, don't give up hope. Reach out to your colleagues and ask them questions. Ask them where else you can get help. One of my favorite online resources is Edutopia.org. The site offers videos, articles, and a community area in which users can start discussions. I've also connected with other online instructors and formed professional learning networks via LinkedIn and Twitter. Even if you are the first instructor to teach online at your institution, you're not the first in the world, and others out there (including me) are willing to help.

1.3 Online Resources

The largest repository of online course development and learning tools is the Internet. Here are some of my favorite Internet resources that are reliable and free:

Cross-Curricular:
- NANSLO (https://wiche.edu/nanslo) stands for North American Network of Science Labs Online, an international consortium that provides access to online lab activities, software, and robotics that allow students to access lab equipment in a remote lab via the Internet to perform experiments.

- OpenStax (https://openstax.org/) is a non-profit source of textbooks and ancillary materials that are free and openly licensed for use in education. The textbooks are available online, and you can apply for an instructor account that will grant you access to the instructor resources.

- PhET (https://phet.colorado.edu/) is a collection of interactive simulations for biology, chemistry, physics, and Earth science that you can search by topic and grade level.

- The University of Oklahoma Libraries have developed a website (http://guides.ou.edu/OER) with open educational resources for biology, chemistry, geology, and physics, along with other topics. The website also has valuable general information about what open educational resources are and copyright information.

Biology:

- Howard Hughes Medical Institute has assembled a large collection of science education resources on their Biointeractive site (https://www.hhmi.org/biointeractive), with a concentration in the life sciences. You can download and use the resources for education, but commercial use requires permission. They are very specific about how you can use their resources on their Terms of Use page (https://www.hhmi.org/terms-of-use). They have lesson plans, in class activities, videos, and even virtual labs, which are research based and high quality. You can search by topic, resource type, or collection, and the grade level and Next Generation Science Standards are attached to each resource.

- The University of Delaware's Virtual Microscope is available under a Creative Commons License (https://www1.udel.edu/biology/ketcham/microscope/scope.html). The Virtual Microscope simulates a binocular compound microscope, allowing control of the oculars, diaphragm, objectives, stage, and focus. It provides a tutorial for how to use the microscope, and is helpful even as just a prelab activity for face-to-face classes.

Chemistry

- The Chemical Education Digital Library (http://www.chemeddl.org/) hosts digital resources for teaching chemistry. Resources are categorized by topic, education level, and application.

Geology

- EarthViewer is an online, interactive tool for exploring the history of Earth from Howard Hughes Medical Institute's Biointeractive (http://www.hhmi.org/biointeractive/earthviewer-online-and-downloadable-version). As you scroll through billions of years, you see how continents moved and changed through time. You can select several data sets to add to your view, like extinction events, carbon dioxide levels, and temperature. EarthViewer is available online, for computer download, or as an app.

- Earth Science World Image Bank (http://www.earthscience-world.org/images/) provides over 6000 searchable geoscience images for use in education. Their Image Use page provides information on acceptable use of the images (http://www.earthscienceworld.org/images/imageuse.html).

- The Digital Library for Earth System Education (DLESE) hosts a collection of activities, searchable by grade level, research type, and standards (http://www.dlese.org/library/index.jsp).

Physics

- The American Association of Physics Teachers has collected physics resources into a searchable website called comPADRE (http://compadre.org/), which has sections devoted to higher education courses and open source physics resources.

CHAPTER 2
GENERAL TIPS & STRATEGIES

2.1 Expect the Unexpected

We could swap stories all day and no two stories would be exactly alike, because no two situations are the same. Hurricane Harvey hit Texas in the summer of 2017, destroying buildings and homes, submerging cities, and killing over 80 people. Some schools and colleges were not able to open on time in August, and some students were not able to make it to their college even if it was able to open. Texas A&M University provided a hotline for students who had trouble reaching campus, and the University of Texas provided an online form for students to notify instructors that they were affected by the storm (Watkins, 2017). While we cannot predict what might happen, we can make some basic preparations. Here are some suggestions.

- Keep a list of names and numbers of whom to call for various needs. Here are a few recommendations:

  Department head

  Mentor

  Instructional designer and/or distance learning department

  Technology help desk

  Internet service provider (you'll also need account info.)

- Provide students with an emergency contact name and number in case they cannot reach you.

- Know your college's policy for giving a student an incomplete.

- Have a backup plan in case your electricity or Internet goes out.

- Download student contact information so you can contact students in case of an Internet or power outage.

If a potential serious situation arises, like a hurricane or other natural disaster, don't just sit and wait to see what happens. Contact your students in advance to make sure they are aware of the situation. They could be in a different area, and not aware or affected, but they still need to know there could be an issue with the course and that you are planning for it. Also, make sure students know to contact you immediately as well if a situation arises in their area.

2.2 Plan to Differentiate for Technological Skill

In 2015, 68 percent of students agreed or strongly agreed that they had adequate preparation to use required technology in their college classes. However, 39 percent did not feel adequately prepared to use specific types of technology used by their institution, like the course registration system, learning management system, or library search function. Additionally, 27 percent of students would have liked more preparation on basic computer software when they entered college (Brooks, 2016). Online instructors cannot assume their students can use technology well. We must build our courses so that differences in technological skill do not become barriers to success.

Consider having your students complete an online readiness survey. MERLOT (www.merlot.org) has a collection of links to surveys prepared by several institutions. Your college may have their own, so check with your distance learning department and/or instructional designer. You can make the survey part of your orientation unit, and require it either as a grade or as a pre-requisite to accessing materials. It's very important to orient students to your learning management system and the course content, but some students might need more help. Reading the student surveys help you identify those students, and the areas in which they are weakest.

For example, the Pennsylvania State University offers an Online Readiness Assessment which asks students to Agree, Somewhat

Agree, or Disagree to statements regarding their self-direction, learning preferences, study habits, technology skills, and computer equipment capabilities. Once the student submits answers, a report is generated that explains the student's score (Williams, 2017). The University of North Carolina at Chapel Hill developed an Online Learning Readiness Questionnaire which gives a more tailored report with links to resources (Online Learning Readiness Questionnaire).

You can eliminate many student questions by providing a solid orientation that explains where to find materials, how to access assignments and grades, and how to submit assignments. (See Chapter 10). However, students will ask you technical questions you had not considered. For example, I require students to submit the certificate that is displayed upon completing the online safety activity. Some students did not know how to take a screenshot, and asked me. I replied by sending links to YouTube video tutorials. After that, I included those links in the FAQ section of my course shell.

You'll be able to answer many of these questions if you learn how to complete the tasks you ask your students to complete. If you want students to submit a video, then you should know at least one way for students to make the video, and how they can upload the video from their phone, iPad, etc. into the learning management system.

For other questions, you'll need to know where to refer students. For example, a student may ask you about a computer problem, and you can refer that student to the college technology help desk. Create a contact list in advance and post it where students (and you) can access it. Some students will find the contact information they need and contact them directly. Others will contact you because they forgot about the contact list or don't know whom on the list they should contact. We have all felt frustrated at some point when dealing with technology, and our students certainly will. Being patient and kind can alleviate everyone's frustration.

2.3 Having your Course Reviewed

Once you have your course built and organized in the LMS, consider asking for your course to be reviewed. It may sound scary, but having a colleague, instructional designer, and/or others look through everything in your course can be extremely helpful. You know what you meant in your instructions, but they may not be as clear to others. Think about how many questions you receive about assignments in your face-to-face classes. Questions in an online class take longer to answer, simply because you and your students are not in the same place at the same time. Suppose a student emailed you a question at 9 p.m. last night, and you read and reply to the email this morning at 9 a.m. 12 hours have already gone by. The student may not read be able to read your answer until that evening, which means potentially 24 hours has gone by before the student receives an answer.

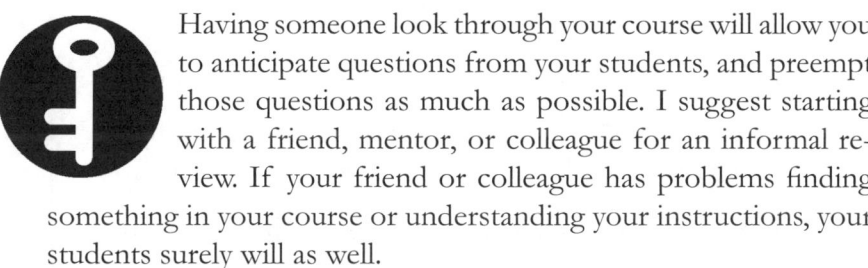 Having someone look through your course will allow you to anticipate questions from your students, and preempt those questions as much as possible. I suggest starting with a friend, mentor, or colleague for an informal review. If your friend or colleague has problems finding something in your course or understanding your instructions, your students surely will as well.

When I developed my first online course, I asked my mentor to review the course. Since we had worked together closely from the beginning of the project, he knew what lessons I had used and was mainly looking at organization and usability. Other colleagues reviewed the course after that. They offered suggestions and asked questions such as how the dropboxes worked, or how I was able to ensure that students completed tasks on time. I asked them for feedback on some specific issues, and I included some suggested questions to ask your reviewers.

Ten questions to ask your course reviewer/colleagues

1. Is there anything in the course that you feel is missing or that you cannot find?

2. Is there anything in the course that you found confusing?

3. Was there anything in the course that you could not access?

4. Are there any broken links?

5. Was there anything that you tried to complete for which you needed to download new software, or that did not work for you?

6. If you were a student in this course, would you know what to complete each week?

7. Do you feel assignment instructions are explicit enough?

8. Do you feel the amount of work/time students complete in the course each week is appropriate?

9. Do you have any ideas about lesson alternatives that might fit well into the course?

10. What questions do you have about the course?

Some colleges have committees that review online and blended courses. Sometimes the review is required, while other times, the review is voluntary. I reviewed some online courses for Blinn College, and at that time, all new blended and online courses were reviewed to ensure that they met minimum standards set by the college. At McLennan Community College, where I teach now, every new blended and online course must go through an approval process to ensure that each course meets the minimum standards set by MCC. They also provide a course that teaches faculty members the basics of the LMS and online course design. It's a very helpful course and provides instructors with the skills and information needed to develop their online course. Each college has its own process of course development and approval, which could include a review process. Don't be scared of the review. No reviewer will disparage your course, but will ask questions and offer suggestions.

Quality Matters

Quality Matters (QM) provides a way to measure the quality of an online course against a rubric of standards for course design through peer review. Faculty are trained to evaluate courses based on the QM rubric, and serve as peer reviewers for college and K-12 courses. Colleges may be members of Quality Matters, which gives college discounts on course reviews, among other benefits. Ask your department head, instructional technologist, and/or your college's Teaching and Learning department if your college is a QM member. If so, ask if the college pays for course reviews. The cost for a QM-managed course review is $1,000 for member institutions. If your college is not a member, you can still have your course reviewed, but the cost goes up to $1,400 (Quality Matters).

The QM review uses the proprietary QM Rubric and tools available to member institutions, and will offer feedback to help improve your course and create a more engaging experience for students. To have the course reviewed, the reviewers must have access to the course, and will use QM rubrics or a custom rubric (depending on the type of review). The number of reviewers also depends on the type of review, but all will be QM-certified. A final report is generated based on the review that gives a score for the overall course quality (Quality Matters).

Once you have developed lessons and built your course in the LMS, a large part of your work is complete. However, you'll never be completely finished, since you will want to update your course at least once a year. Consider the feedback you receive from students and build on your strengths. You can try a new strategy each semester in place of one that was weak (Strandberg and Campbell, 2014).

CHAPTER 3
THE PEDAGOGY YOU NEED TO SUCCEED

This chapter is adapted from "The Keys to Online Learning for Adults: The Six Principles of Andragogy," by Wendy Conaway and Barbara Zorn-Arnold, published in *Distance Learning For Educators, Trainers, and Leaders*, vol. 12 no. 4, 2015.

3.1 Adult Learning Principles

1. The Learner's Prior Experience

We must respect the diversity of the learners in our courses and provide activities that build on their prior knowledge and experience. Older students are likely to have more experience than younger students, but even college students fresh out of high school will have some experience, both physical and psychological (Conaway and Zorn-Arnold, 2015). College science instructors can increase students' experience by providing laboratory activities, and experience from other types of activities. Students will integrate these experiences with their past learning, each interpreting and applying the knowledge slightly differently. Instructors must embrace these differences in experiences and allow students to share and learn from each other.

2. The Learner's Self-Concept

Adults make independent decisions and accept consequences of their actions. This self-directed behavior is a large part of the self-concept of adult learners. Adult students like to feel in control over their learning. Online courses hold immense potential in this regard, since adult learners can truly embrace their autonomy.

3. The Learner's Need to Know

Students enroll in classes for distinct reasons, which can all typically be traced back to their desire to learn. Perhaps a student is in your class because they wish to major in science, improve their skills to further their career, or simply because they realize they cannot graduate without that specific credit. Adult students may question why they need to take a specific course or learn about a specific topic within a course. Instructors need to help students answer this important question.

4. The Learner's Readiness to Learn

Returning, non-traditional students who voluntarily enroll in classes are typically ready to put in the work to get the outcome they desire. You will likely have some of these types of students in your classes, and you can leverage their experience with younger, traditional students. I usually ask students to share advice and study tips, and find that students are more likely to listen to other students in this regard than to me.

5. The Learner's Orientation to Learning

Adult learners want to know how what they are learning will benefit them. How will this help them in their career? How will this apply to their lives? In this way, their orientation to learning is centered on solving problems.

6. The Learner's Motivation

You cannot force a student to learn, so intrinsic motivation is vital for adult students. Adult students are attending college because they want to be there, and it is helpful to know their reasons to better connect with them.

It is important to understand that our students will have diverse levels of experience, self-directedness and motivation. Some students may be more ready to learn than others, and we cannot ignore those who are not as ready. We must build in flexibility and student support to accommodate for these differences.

3.2 Best Practices in Undergraduate Education

In 1987, Chickering and Gamson developed Seven Principles of Good Practice in Undergraduate Education (Chickering and Gamson). Multiple studies have demonstrated the efficacy of these principles, and they have been applied to online education (Guidera, 2003-2004; Zhang and Walls, 2006; Hathaway, 2014). The Seven Principles are described below, along with how they apply to online education.

1. Good practice encourages contact between students and faculty.

Communication is a major theme throughout this book. Online students may be physically alone when they work on course material, but we don't want them to feel alone when taking our courses. Frequent communication between students and faculty are essential for student motivation and involvement in classes. We want students to feel like they can ask questions, make comments, and get help when needed. However, from my experience, not all students in online classes feel this way. Often, early in the semester, when I receive an email or phone call from a student, the conversation begins with the student apologizing for bothering me. I always make a point to let them know it is no bother, but I can't help but wonder what prior experience led to this. I then send a reminder to all my students that I am here to help and they should feel free to ask me questions. We will discuss contact between students and faculty in multiple sections of this book, including an entire chapter on keeping in touch with your students and building learning communities (Chapter 11).

2. Good practice develops reciprocity and cooperation among students.

Students in online classes often miss out on the opportunities to get to know their classmates. There are no virtual hallways in which students can meet and chat about the latest movie or music release. We must help our online students become a community of learners that share and build knowledge together. Students become more involved in learning when they work as a team to master course material, discussing ideas and activating deeper thinking. We can use discussion forums and collaborative activities to facilitate this, which are both discussed in detail in Chapter 7.

3. Good practice uses active learning techniques.

Active learning occurs when students relate information to their own lives, process and think deeply about it, and construct their own knowledge. We can use discussion forums and collaborative activities to facilitate this, which are both discussed in detail in Chapter 7.

4. Good practice gives prompt feedback.

Feedback helps students know what they know and don't know, and how they can improve their performance. After multiple opportunities to perform and receive feedback, students can begin to self-assess and reflect on their learning. Formative assessments (discussed more in Chapter 13) allow instructors to gather data about how students are progressing and give them feedback.

5. Good practice emphasizes time on task.

Time and energy are investments for students and teachers which lead to learning. More investment leads to more payoff. We begin our discussion of time on task in this chapter (3) by emphasizing that faculty allot the time required to build an engaging, rigorous online science course. We'll come back to time on task in Chapters 8 and 12 when we discuss time management.

6. Good practice communicates high expectations.

When you expect more, you tend to get more in return. This applies to teachers and students. You should have high expectations of yourself and your students. High expectations are communicated in several ways, from the very first day of the course. Emphasizing that students can do well in the course, and helping them get oriented to your online course, will help them be successful. We'll discuss orienting students to your course in Chapter 10. In Chapter 7, we'll also discuss course and lesson learning objectives, which must clearly communicate your learning expectations.

7. Good practice respects diverse talents and ways of learning.

Building a learning community helps everyone respect each other's strengths and learning styles. Facilitating communication between students can help with this, because they can begin to learn from each other. Some students may be strong in one area of a course, but struggle in another. A student may not learn well from reading the textbook, while another may not be able to listen to a lecture and pull out vital material. Having a variety of learning activities can help all students, and we'll cover that in the first part of Chapter 7.

3.3 Investing Your Time Up Front

Now is the time for some hard truths. Fewer than 30 percent of academic leaders surveyed in 2015 reported that their faculty saw online education as valuable and legitimate (Allen, et al., 2016). Some instructors think that teaching online is a snap and/or that online instructors are always off on vacation somewhere, teaching from the beach. However, creating rigorous and engaging science courses for an online platform takes time. The reality is this: an online instructor will invest significant time in course preparation, grading, and student communication. Teaching science online – particularly with migrating an existing face-to-face course to an online learning management system (LMS) or online format – requires a more substantial time commitment than teaching a course face-to-face.

 The fifth Principle of Good Practice (PGP) emphasizes time on task, for students and instructors. Be sure to allocate realistic amounts of time for planning, building, and facilitating your course.

When I built my first online class, I spent the first week (20-30 hours) of summer planning my course organization, identifying learning goals, organizing the calendar, and gathering resources. Over the next two weeks, I reviewed lab materials and selected lessons to include in my online course. The rest of the summer I spent preparing audio and video recordings of course materials for my students, writing instructions, and building the course in the LMS. In total, I spent 9-10 weeks that summer planning and creating my online biology course. At 20-30 hours per week, this leads to an estimate of 180 – 300 hours to plan and create a quality online course. This does not include the time I spent with colleagues the following fall semester to demonstrate and discuss the course, or time spent on reviewing the course with an instructional designer.

A study published in the *Online Journal of Distance Learning Administration* found that, "developing online courses is indeed more time consuming than developing face-to-face courses. Though the time required declines when the same instructor develops a second or third online course. Twenty-nine percent of respondents indicated they spend over 100 hours (median of 70 hours) to develop their (first) online course" (Freeman, 2015). Though respondents in the survey reported that teaching online took more time than teaching face-to-face, by the third time facilitating an online course, respondents noted that it took them about the same amount of time as it did a similar face-to-face course. Freeman (2015) writes:

There is supporting evidence to the earlier finding that teaching an online course the second and third time becomes about as time-consuming as teaching a face-to-face course the second and third time. The factors that still remain more time-consuming for online teaching compared with face-to-face teaching, even after teaching the course three times, are Instructor-Student Interaction and Grading & Assessment, the two specific factors that can not be prepared in advance for online courses (unlike Content Development and Pre-Semester Setup) or likely occur equally across all courses in all modes (Overall Involvement in the Class).

A startling (and significant) finding of this study concerns the time dedicated to grading and assessing online students. Freeman's data (2015) reveal that time dedicated to grading students' work increased from the first to third time of facilitating an online course. Two-thirds of the respondents indicated by the third time it took "somewhat more," "more," or "much more" time to grade and assess students in an online course than face-to-face. These results are actually encouraging, since an instructor's feedback to students about course work can motivate students, deepen their knowledge, and help them to think critically (Getzlaf, et. al., 2009). There are several technology tools and applications which can help instructors to achieve efficiency and make the most of giving feedback using online tools that deliver meaningful, quality feedback for students.

The Center for Educational Innovation at the University of Minnesota tells instructors it will take six to nine months to develop an online course, even if the instructor has already taught the course in a face-to-face setting (Center for Educational Innovation). How much time you spend developing your course will determine the quality and rigor of the course. The Center for Educational Innovation provides estimates of hours required to develop online courses based on three models. Simply uploading content for online delivery requires approximately 60-80 hours. Restructuring and organizing content specifically for online delivery, which could include the assistance of an instructional designer, requires 160-280 hours. Creating rich, engaging experiences for students requires 300-600 hours (Center for Educational Innovation). The wide range of time depends on several factors:

- Whether you have assistance in course design and uploading materials.

- The types of instructional strategies you use in your courses.

- How proficient and comfortable you are with technology and your learning management system.

- The amount of material typically covered in your course.

- Whether your course includes labs.

- How much assistance your college provides instructors in building online courses.

Developing a quality online course is challenging. In addition, there is an interdependent relationship between technology and andragogy specific to online courses. For example, the features of a LMS platform will determine and shape the course and the teaching methods. In addition to time, online course design requires skills that include not only familiarity with LMS features, but also outside tools including social media platforms that can enhance student learning. Knowledge of user-focused design, or web design principles is also important in delivering an intuitive learning experience for students.

Your goal is to build a rigorous and engaging online course in which students can master the course materials and succeed, not to rush through and upload files into the LMS. Up front planning makes a difference in how effective you and your lessons are in facilitating student learning. That being said, it is important to remember that your upfront time investment will pay off in the long run, since you'll spend less time on student questions, rewriting instructions, and looking for alternative lessons while facilitating subsequent sections of the course.

The quality of your course planning greatly impacts the quality of your interactions with students in online science courses. At Blinn College, I participated in peer reviews of online courses. Reviews of well-planned courses went very quickly, since course materials were easy to find, all the links and media worked as expected, instructions were clear, and due dates were obvious. In a few courses, however, I was confused about assignments, could not find dropboxes, or otherwise found it difficult to navigate the course. I remember one course we had to decline to review because there was not even enough material in the course for us to critique. In a poorly planned online course, instructors will spend inordinate amounts of time answering the same questions repeatedly because students cannot find, access, or understand instructions for assignments.

Invest upfront time and you won't have to find materials, convert them to online lessons, and insert them into your learning management system (LMS) while also answering clarifying questions about course material, engaging students in discussions, and grading assignments. Investing time up front to have a complete, well-organized course before students begin the semester will make your teaching semester much less stressful and more fun for you and your students.

I know that the nine months that went into planning, developing, and reviewing that first biology course was well-invested. Why? The class filled very quickly after registration opened and there was a wait list. There were a few broken links to fix, some Internet issues, and some unforeseen problems, but students were successful.

Below is a comparison of my first fully online course from Spring 2014 (first semester introductory biology for science majors) with a face-to-face section of the same course from the same semester. As you see from the data below, there was little difference in student retention, and only a slightly larger difference in passing final grades between the online section and face-to-face sections.

Face-to-Face Biology 1406	**Fully Online Biology 1406**
Beginning Enrollment: 27	Beginning Enrollment: 28
Ending Enrollment: 21	Ending Enrollment: 21
Total Passed: 17 (80.9%)	Total Passed: 16 (76.2%)

The numbers above are a snapshot of one science class in one semester. Data on retention of students in online classes in general, reveals that face-to-face classes have higher retention rates (Carr, 2000). A more recent study compared students in online courses against those enrolled in face-to-face sections of the same course taught by the same professor. Completion rates in the online sections were slightly lower (93.3 percent) than face-to-face (95.6 percent) (Atchley, Wingenbach and Akers, 2013).

The completion rates in both my online and my face-to-face classes are significantly lower than those in the Atchley study, but that is likely due to a difference in subject. From 2003-2009, 69 percent of Science, Technology, Engineering, and Math (STEM) majors in U.S. Associate's Degree programs had either dropped out of college or changed major (Chen, 2013). The difference could also represent differences in how universities report their completion rates, making data comparing completion rates across universities difficult to interpret. Some universities include those students who drop courses during the add/drop days at the first of the semester in the numbers, which would make their drop rates significantly higher than those universities which only count students who drop after the state census date (Carr, 2000).

3.4 Course Ownership

Before I built my first fully online introductory biology course at Blinn College, I submitted a proposal to the Vice President of Academic Affairs to be paid to design the course in lieu of teaching one summer session course. It was my understanding that the course I built could then be used as a course shell in the future for other instructors. However, there was nothing specific regarding course ownership in my agreement with the college to develop the course. Your college may pay you to design a course, but be aware that if your college pays you, that course could become the institution's property. Make sure any contract or agreement you sign with your college specifies information about course ownership and licenses for use.

Be aware that even if your college does *not* pay you to plan and build a course, the college could still assert ownership rights. In a survey of 110 colleges and universities, over one-third claimed university ownership of faculty developed online courses, even if the college did not pay faculty for course development (Butrymowicz, 2014). In 2012, two former professors at Arizona State University sued their college for using an online course they'd developed without the professors' permission (Basu, 2012), but their case was later dismissed in federal court (Butrymowicz, 2014).

Just the opposite occurred with the online course I built. After a reorganization of the college's administration structure, the new department leadership decided to discontinue the course. It is difficult to predict how a college will use online courses, so ask questions and read all paperwork so you know what to expect before you invest your time. Although policies and procedures will vary from college to college, typically, in any course development contract or proposal, information about the following items are included:

- Time-line for development and implementation of the course

- Payment or other compensation

- Minimum course standards or specifications regarding content

- Ownership of course materials

- Licenses granted for the college's use of the course

- Copyright information for any 3rd party materials

- Allowed outside use by the course developer

- Required training or qualifications for course developer

CHAPTER 4
TEXTBOOKS/ONLINE HOMEWORK SYSTEMS

4.1 To Textbook or Not to Textbook?

 I'll let you in on a little secret: I don't always require students to purchase the textbook in my classes. For several reasons I leave the decision up to each student. Several studies have shown that many science students simply do not read the assigned textbook (Burton, 2014; Podolefsky and Finkelstein, 2006). In a study of physics students, Podolefsky and Finkelstein reported that 97 percent of their introductory physics students purchased the textbook, but only 37 percent of students said they actually read it (2006). A study in 2014 reported that less than half of students completed reading assignments at the beginning of the semester, and after mid-term, that number had dropped to less than 10 percent (Burton).

Studies have shown little correlation between grades and how often students read the textbook (Burton, 2014; Podolefsky and Finkelstein, 2006; French, et al., 2015). French, et al. analyzed textbook use in 12 science courses, and found that students who said they often read the textbook earned higher course averages than students who said they sometimes read the textbook. However, students who said they rarely read the textbook earned higher grades than students who read often or sometimes (French, et al., 2015). Two groups of students seem to emerge: those who earn higher grades by reading the textbook, and those who don't. I always encouraged my students to purchase the textbook if they would use it, but many students told me that they bought books they never even opened. For those students, purchasing a textbook would have been a waste of money, especially when you consider textbook prices.

For many students, the cost of textbooks can become a burden. Textbook prices have increased 73 percent since 2006, with only 5 publishers controlling 80 percent of the market (Senack and Donoghue, 2016). With such little competition, it should not be surprising that prices have increased so dramatically. Students have no input about what textbook to purchase, so they must somehow figure out how to pay for their required materials. Textbook publishers market their materials to colleges and instructors like pharmaceutical companies market medications to hospitals and doctors (Popken, 2017), but there is no insurance to cover the costs of textbooks. Almost 30 percent of students use financial aid to cover the cost of textbooks, and typically, the amount that is covered by financial aid each semester is at least $300 (Senack and Donoghue, 2016). On average, undergraduate students at public colleges pay almost $1,300 per year for textbooks (Quick Guide: College Costs). What if a student does not have enough money and/or financial aid to cover the cost of their textbooks?

 Some students may be affected more by the high cost of textbooks than others. When we break down the 30 percent of students who use financial aid for textbooks, 50 percent of them are enrolled in community or two-year colleges (Senack and Donoghue, 2016). Fortunately, community and two-year colleges offer lower tuition and fees than 4-year public and private universities, which is a large incentive to choose them (Mitchell, 2015; Grinberg, Gumbrecht and Patterson, 2014; Kolesnikova, 2009). However, the money saved on tuition and fees could be offset by the cost of required materials. Students who choose community colleges because of cost would be harder hit by the prohibitive cost of textbooks.

Don't require assignments based solely on reading the textbook. I also did not require reading quizzes. If you do any of these, you obviously will require students to purchase and read the textbook. In these cases, in which a portion of the grade average results directly from textbook based assignments, it is no surprise that students who read the textbook often earned higher grades. What is surprising, is that students who reported never reading the textbook in these courses scored higher than those who said they read the textbook often (French, et al., 2015). Knowing this, instructors must consider whether requiring that students purchase a textbook is really worth the money students will spend.

4.2 Textbook Format Options

If your college requires you to use a textbook, students should have choice in format and retailer. First, we'll discuss format options. Younger students, those who are on financial aid or scholarships, and science majors are all more likely to choose e-textbooks. In addition, students who own a laptop or desktop are more likely to use e-textbooks (Miller, Nutting and Baker-Eveleth, 2013), so e-textbooks should be an option for them.

For others, print copies may be preferable. In a study, participants who had never used an e-textbook stated a preference for print textbooks for assorted reasons, including eyestrain when trying to read on an electronic screen, difficulty reading on a small electronic device, limited attention span, and technological difficulties (deNoyelles, Raible and Seilhamer, 2016).

Perhaps you personally like to use print copies of textbooks for these or other reasons. You can still allow students a choice of print copy or e-textbook. Generally, the electronic version exactly matches the print version, but a few students have reported that either their instructor advised them to specifically purchase the print copy of the textbook or did not explicitly state that the electronic version of the textbook was acceptable. In that same survey, only around 10% of students reported never using an e-textbook in a college course (deNoyelles, Raible and Seilhamer, 2016).

Students who use e-textbooks benefit from the search feature and integrated glossary. They can highlight and make notes in the e-textbook, just like in the print version, and in some cases, instructors can make notes and annotate sections for students as well. Does the format of the textbook really matter, if students benefit from it? In an online class, this question becomes even more relevant. Students are taking class online, so why shouldn't their textbook be online as well? Considering the mix of preferences for print versus eBooks, it makes sense to offer students a choice of purchasing their preferred version.

You can determine the options available to students in several ways. The college bookstore is a place to start. They will provide new and used options of print copies, access codes for e-textbooks, or perhaps even rent print or e-textbooks. The textbook sales representative can give you information, along with alternative purchasing options for students who are not on campus and cannot make it to the college bookstore. Many students purchase textbooks through the college bookstore and an online retailer (McGowan and Stephens, 2015), so check online to see what is available for students. Provide students information about all their options, and let them choose what is best for them.

4.3 Open Educational Resources

If your college allows flexibility in what textbook you choose, you'll want to consider open educational resources. Open textbooks are licensed under copyright licenses, like Creative Commons, that allow use, if users follow the guidelines outlined in the license. Generally, open textbooks are freely available in electronic format, and print copies may be available for a nominal fee. The wonderful thing about open textbooks is that instructors can customize the material for their courses (Open Textbook 101). There are several resources you can use to find open textbooks for use in your courses, some of which are described here.

- B.C. Open Textbook Collection (https://open.bccampus.ca/ find-open-textbooks/) provides links to open textbooks, sorted by discipline. Each link is accompanied by a description of the textbook, whether it has been reviewed by faculty, and whether there are any ancillary materials associated with the book (Open Textbook 101). License information is also included, so you know exactly what uses are allowed.

- A similar collection of open textbooks is maintained by the University of Minnesota's Center for Open Education. The Open Textbook Library (https://open.umn.edu/opentextbooks/)

hosts open textbooks that can be downloaded, accessed online, or printed for a nominal charge. The textbooks in this library are used at by colleges or associated with a college, scholarly society, or professional organization (Open Textbook Library).

- OpenStax (www.OpenStax.com) offers a collection of open education resources, which have been reviewed and used by faculty in college courses. OpenStax resources include textbooks, ancillary materials, and in some cases, online learning, practice, and assessment resources. For example, WileyPLUS has integrated materials from the OpenStax college biology textbook and created an online system that creates a personalized learning experience for students at a reduced cost (John Wiley & Sons, Inc., 2013).

- The Orange Grove (https://florida.theorangegrove.org/og/home.do) is Florida's Open Educational Resource Repository, which includes higher education resources. Instructors can rate and comment on resources as well, a feature not found in all other collections.

- MERLOT (https://www.merlot.org/merlot/index.htm) houses a collection of learning resources contributed by members of the MERLOT community, who have either created or discovered materials created by others, and shared them.

The increase in open educational resources, coupled with online learning, opens the higher education door to students who would otherwise not be able to attend college due to location and financial issues. The quality of open textbooks is increasing as well, with many of them being peer reviewed. As more features are added for lower cost, textbook publishers may face pressure to lower costs themselves.

Lower cost is not our only concern. Instructors must ensure that they choose materials of sufficient quality that learning is not compromised. In one study, over 95 percent of instructors surveyed stated that, since using OpenStax college textbooks, they were more likely to recommend them to colleagues. After integrating OpenStax resources into their courses, educators reported increased participation of students (Pitt, 2015). This increased participation suggests that OpenStax resources are not simply low-cost, but also high quality.

A study published in 2016 found that in general, students met the same learning goals using open educational resources as when using commercial textbooks. This suggests that open educational resources do not decrease learning, but the authors of the study note that how learning resources are used could make a difference in student learning (Hilton, 2016).

 A pattern emerges: the instructor plays a huge role in facilitating learning, regardless of the format of the course, or the resources used in the course. You are vital to the success of your course.

4.4 Online Homework Systems

Science textbooks from commercial textbook publishers often have an accompanying online homework system. Each will be slightly different, and offer different levels of interaction for students, but they all offer some benefits to students and instructors: decreased grading time, immediate feedback to students, and a potential to identify students who need extra help (Perdian, 2013).

Instructors like online homework systems because the computer software grades the questions (Perdian, 2013). Instructors save time by not having to grade everything by hand. In some cases, the online homework system will integrate with your learning management system (LMS), which means that the grades automatically transfer from the online homework system to the gradebook. We'll discuss learning management systems more in Chapter 6.

For students, online homework systems offer immediate feedback (Perdian, 2013). Principles of Good Practice emphasize prompt feedback (Chickering and Gamson, 1987), so online learning systems support this principle. Using feedback from the homework system, students learn from their mistakes (Butler and Zerr, 2005).

Multiple studies have demonstrated that online homework systems can raise students' exam scores (Bowman, Gulacar and King, 2014; Marorell and McIntire, 2011; Sundaram and Roberts, 2015; Wu and Cheng, 2015; Butler and Zerr, 2005). A study in 2005 revealed that students who utilized an online homework system in a mathematics class scored better on exams (Butler and Zerr, 2005). In 2015, students using SaplingLearning in an economics class showed increases in essay scores, midterm and final exam grades, and attendance rates (Wu and Cheng, 2015). Another study demonstrated that online homework systems can improve student performance on application activities (Sundaram and Roberts, 2015).

 **If you choose to use an online homework system, always use data from the system to identify and help struggling students.**

In a 2013 study, instructors were able to identify which students were underperforming and overperforming by analyzing data from an online homework system. Underperforming students in the study spent more time on online homework, but earned lower scores. Overperforming students spent less time on online homework, but earned higher scores (Perdian, 2013). You can look at student data in an online homework system to see which students are randomly guessing at answers, determine which students may be struggling, and which topics are more difficult for students overall (Bowman, Gulacar and King, 2014). Instructors could use this data to refer students to services like tutoring (Perdian, 2013).

In science courses, students have different backgrounds and prior knowledge, and online homework systems can help them grow their knowledge and understanding regardless of their differing prior knowledge (Marorell and McIntire, 2011). Students in this study noted that the online homework system was more helpful when the class topics (lecture and textbook readings) more closely aligned with the online homework. Some also complained that the online homework system was too picky with regard to the answer format, and that sometimes the questions had confusing wording (Marorell and McIntire, 2011).

Electronic versions of textbooks are often sold packaged with online access to the textbook's online homework system, so students will have that resource as well. If students purchase used hard copies of textbooks, they will then need to purchase online access separately. I have found, though, that a student can purchase access to the online homework system along with an electronic version of the textbook for less than the cost of a new hard copy of the textbook alone. Another benefit of the eBook is that those students who choose to use the electronic version of the textbook that comes with the online learning system don't have to carry around the heavy print copy of the textbook.

Online learning platforms have come a long way over the past few years. I recently attended a publisher's overview of their textbook and online learning platform, and was pleasantly surprised by what I saw. Everything was customizable for each class, and even for each student. You can differentiate for each student through their online system! That's perfect for online classes. I don't know if every online learning system will do this, but it's something to consider. Call or email your textbook sales rep and ask if they will give you an overview of their system in person or online. There is usually a contact form and phone number on the website for the publisher, and they'll be happy to give you the information for your sales representative and/or pass along your contact information. In the 45-minute overview I mentioned earlier, I learned so much more than I could going through the system by myself. It's worth a phone call or email to see if they can help you.

 If you use an online homework system, advise students on strategies to increase their retention and success in the course.

The efficacy of an online homework system depends on individual student and instructor use. A study of an online homework system found a correlation between how students interacted with the material could predict success in the course. Taking time to find the correct answer to a question is more effective in learning the material than repeatedly guessing at answers (Bowman, Gulacar and King, 2014). However, the amount of time spent on online homework does not necessarily correlate to improved performance. Procrastinators who start and submit assignments late do not perform well, while students who start and submit assignments early tend to perform better (Mo, 2015). In online courses, this is especially relevant. Instructors must encourage students to start assignments early and not procrastinate. More about procrastination will be covered in Chapter 12.

You'll need to carefully go through the online homework system to determine if you think it will be useful for your course and worth the cost to the student for access. For an online course, it can be a great asset, since it will save you time as opposed to building assignments and tutorials yourself. Another benefit of carefully going through the online system yourself is that you can help guide students through the system. If you don't take the time to learn and use the features of the textbook/website, your students won't either. When setting up your course in the LMS, add an orientation to the eBook and online learning system. Making a screencast video of you going through the features will greatly help students as they begin to use the system, and keep you from having to answer redundant questions. Make sure to point out specific items you want students to access and other things you think will benefit them.

Going through all the resources that textbook publishers offer will be time consuming, but worth it. You'll be able to choose appropriate assignments. You'll also want to know what animations and videos are available as alternatives to lecture. You won't use everything provided with the textbook, and you'll want to supplement with other resources. When developing your course, you should include resources that support your instruction, rather than trying to match your instruction to a textbook.

CHAPTER 5
CHOOSING LABORATORY ACTIVITIES

5.1 Labs or No Labs?

Not every science course requires a lab component, and some majors do not require students to take the lab portion of science courses. The Texas Core Curriculum no longer requires the lab component of science electives; it now only requires six hours of science rather than eight (Texas Core Curriculum). Some college majors still require the lab portion of science courses, though, and perhaps for good reason. Lab activities allow students to experience science rather than simply reading and discussing scientific information. This levels the field for students with diverse backgrounds and supports learning for all students, regardless of prior knowledge (Eisenkraft, 2013).

Teaching a lab course online is challenging, but with innovative technology and resources, that challenge is manageable. There are several issues to consider, including how students will obtain access to necessary chemicals and equipment, how instructors can ensure students know how to properly complete experiments, how instructors can reduce their liability in case of accidents or negligence by the student, and perhaps most importantly, student safety. At Blinn College, we considered separating credit for lecture and lab to overcome this issue. By separating the courses, students could take the lecture portion of lab online, and attend once a week for lab. Ultimately, we decided against this option, since not all students who enroll in the online course would be able to attend labs on campus.

Assuming you (or your college) want to include labs in your online course, there are generally four options available. You could have students purchase a lab kit from a supply company, write labs that can be completed at home with everyday items, use virtual simulations, utilize a remote laboratory like NANSLO, or a combination of these options. You should carefully consider your choice, as it could affect your and/or your college's liability in the case of accident or injury.

5.2 Lab Kit Companies

A popular option is to utilize a lab kit supply company. There are several, and your college may already have a contract with one or more of them. Check with your department head to determine if there is already a contract in place. When working with a lab kit company, decide which experiments you would like to use in your course. Pick and choose which experiments you would like students to complete for your course, and the company packages kits specifically for your students. Students then order the kits directly from the company.

There are several advantages to this option. First, students conduct hands-on experiments as they would in a face-to-face class, so they gain experience in using laboratory equipment. Second, the company includes a lab manual with all instructions and safety information. Finally, and perhaps most importantly, is the issue of liability. You can't watch over your online students as they complete a lab activity, so you cannot ensure their safety as well as in a face-to-face class. However, since students purchase lab kits directly from a separate company instead of the instructor or the college, this could mitigate the liability of the college and instructor. For example, in an article of InsideHigherEd.com posted in 2009, Linda Jeschofnig, president and chief executive of HandsOn Labs, writes that, "The liability is ours, and we're happy to accept it because we believe we have a safe product" (Moltz, 2009).

There are three popular companies that offer lab kits for a variety of college science courses. Contact them for sample lab kits to determine which would best meet your needs.

Hands-On Labs
Phone: 866-206-0773
info@holscience.com

eScience Labs
Call us: (888) ESL-KITS
info@esciencelabs.com

Carolina Biological
Phone: (800) 334-5551
www.carolina.com

5.3 Instructor-Written Labs Using Household Materials

Writing your own labs for students to complete at home is difficult. You must consider what chemicals are available to students and safety concerns with instructor-written labs are more of an issue, depending on your subject area. Designing labs will require more time on your part as well, since you would have to write the labs according to what chemicals and supplies are readily available in multiple locations. This would limit your selection of materials and equipment drastically.

Your college could also build its own kit, although the logistics of this could become a nightmare depending on chemicals and equipment used. Your college (you) would have to compile the chemicals, materials and equipment into a kit, and ensure that there are enough kits for all students. Then, the college would have to calculate the costs of the kits so that those costs could be added as fees for students to pay, including shipping. Then the kits would have to be shipped to the students. At Blinn College, it was decided not to develop our own kit for students to purchase.

Instead, we developed our own lab manuals for introductory biology. One goal in developing an online course was to make the online course as similar in content to the face-to-face course as possible. For us, this meant replicating experiments from that lab manual in a format that cost as little extra as possible for students. While the course was successful (see data from chapter 3), I don't recommend this option. An at home lab with materials purchased from local stores could not replicate everything we did in the college laboratory, and some students struggled to find appropriate materials for certain labs. This meant we had to supplement these kitchen labs with online simulations. I used free, open source simulations, which meant that over time, links would break, and I would be forced to rewrite labs and/or find alternative resources, sometimes during the semester.

I was also concerned about my students completing the labs safely. While I had no reports of student accidents, the potential was there. Students could have purchased incorrect materials, mixed incorrect amounts, or made any number of other errors. Since the labs used materials purchased over the counter at local stores, the college felt that risk was low. As the instructor of the course, however, I felt more exposed to liability. Considering the issues of time to write and modify labs to use everyday materials, availability of materials, how well labs using everyday materials can replicate lab experiments, and student safety, having students purchase a lab kit or access to high quality virtual labs seems a more efficient and effective alternative.

5.4 Virtual Labs

There are several advantages of using virtual labs (computer simulations) in your online course, but research suggests that once again, the success in terms of student engagement and learning depends on how the simulations are used in the course. Perhaps most importantly, students can perform experiments in computer simulations that would otherwise be too dangerous to complete outside a supervised classroom laboratory. Computer simulations can also transcend time and space, allowing students to complete simulations of experiments that in real life would be impractical due to time, expense, or lack of equipment. Simulations allows students to experience real-world applications that would otherwise not be available to them (Sahin, 2006).

For example, there are several virtual lab activities from Howard Hughes Medical Institute's Biointeractive (http://www.hhmi.org/biointeractive) website that I have used in my courses. One analyzes the data collected on anole lizards in the Caribbean to determine why there are so many distinct species and how they evolved (http://www.hhmi.org/biointeractive/lizard-evolution-virtual-lab). I could not take students there to study lizards in person (though I would have loved to go), but students could analyze data collected from real scientists in the field. My students learned about evolution, and how different selective pressures affect evolution of species from this lab. Another of their virtual labs allows students to analyze pelvic structures of stickleback fish to learn how data collection and analysis can be used to study evolutionary processes (http://www.hhmi.org/biointeractive/stickleback-evolution-virtual-lab). My students really like the labs, since they deal with real-world data from actual scientists studying these processes.

There are other free resources for simulations as well, but no free resource I have found has a comprehensive set of virtual labs for my course. If you want a comprehensive set of virtual labs from one source, you'll probably need to review virtual lab systems that charge a fee paid by the student. Late Nite Labs has created a set of online laboratory investigations that students access through the Internet after purchasing an access code. They compare the labs to flight simulators, a place in which students can learn and perform experiments without risk of harm to themselves, other students, or property. In a survey of Late Nite Labs users, almost 90% of those surveyed indicated that they liked not having to worry about making mistakes, wasting materials, or causing a potentially danger-ous situation. Late Nite Labs notes that students can even make enough mistakes to cause an explosion in their virtual lab (Schwab, 2012-2013), something we all hope would never happen in real life.

The instructor's side of Late Nite Labs allows you to see infor-mation students' have saved, including each student's experiment log and assignment. The instructor can then post a grade for the student to view, or re-assign the lab if the instructor feels like the student should go through it again (Schwab, 2012-2013). One thing you should investigate is whether the grading system of Late Nite Labs or other online lab company will integrate well into your learning management system. I have seen some outside resources that link with the LMS and automatically populate grades, and others that do not. For resources that do not link directly, you would have to manually enter grades for those assignments.

You may find that your textbook publisher offers virtual simulations to accompany their textbook. Call your textbook sales representative for more information. The lab kit companies mentioned above might also have some online simulations to accompany their kits. For example, a microscope would be too expensive to include in a lab kit, so an online simulation would be a suitable alternative. You should also contact Late-Nite Labs for trial access to their simulations.

Late-Nite Labs
800-262-0518
mlls@macmillan.com

5.5 North American Network of Science Labs Online (NANSLO)

One resource bears special attention: the North American Network of Science Labs Online (NANSLO - http://www.wiche. edu/nanslo). NANSLO offers complete lab manuals for biology and chemistry, and a few lab activities for physics that are openly licensed and customizable, and students can complete experiments by remotely controlling equipment in the NANSLO lab. When I first heard about this resource, I thought it sounded amazing. The more I learned about it, the more excited I became. I felt like Gollum with the One Ring, "My Precious," except, of course, that I am willing to share. Remotely operated labs are the future of online science education!

Here's how the process works. You, the instructor, reserve a block of time through NANSLO's scheduling system for students to complete a NANSLO laboratory activity. The reservation generates a PIN and URL for students to use to schedule a day and time (within the block you reserved) to complete the activity. During their scheduled time, students connect to the NANSLO lab via the Internet and access real laboratory equipment to collect real data, conduct experiments, generate graphs and data tables, capture images, and collaborate with classmates and NANSLO lab personnel. Rather than simple simulations, students are controlling actual laboratory equipment, often too expensive to be included in a lab kit, by remote control via the Internet. And, they are working with actual lab personnel at NANSLO, not a tutorial on a computer screen. This brings the online student as close as possible to the real-life, in-person laboratory as possible in a remote setting (Western Interstate Commission for Higher Education, 2015).

Considering that more and more scientists are using remote technology and robots in their work, and the growth of remote laboratories around the world, students using NANSLO resources are arguably better prepared for advanced science laboratory courses. Technavio estimates that the market for virtual and remote laboratories in the United States will increase by 36 percent, and in Europe by 37% by 2020. The market's growth is influenced by cooperation between educational and other institutions, allowing students and staff of one institution to access remote laboratories of others, thereby supporting more distance education and online courses (Technavio, 2016).

5.6 Effectiveness of Online and At-Home Laboratory Activities

Despite the expansion of online science courses across the world, some faculty and administrators still question how well students can learn science in fully online classes. Most debate centers around the laboratory portion. Can students learn the information and techniques needed to progress into upper level science courses in four-year universities? There is not a wealth of research since fully online science courses are not as widespread as face-to-face courses, but a study shows no significant difference in student learning and preparation for upper level science courses between online courses and face-to-face courses. Since 2001, the Colorado Community College System (CCCS) has offered fully online science courses with the lab portion of the course delivered through commercially available lab kits purchased by students (Epper, 2012). Even though grades received by students in face-to-face science classes were generally higher than those in online science courses, the online students had higher GPAs overall, and more cumulative credit hours completed at the community college.

The Colorado study didn't stop there. Students who transferred from CCCS schools to the University of Colorado (CU) Boulder, CU Colorado Springs, CU Denver, and Colorado State University at Fort Collins were tracked, and were compared based on overall GPA and science major GPA. There was no statistical difference in the GPAs of students who had taken online science courses versus face-to-face courses at community colleges, suggesting that online science courses can prepare students for upper level courses just as well as face-to-face courses (Epper, 2012).

Clearly, commercially available lab kits used in online science courses are effective for student learning, but online simulations can be effective as well. For students who have grown up in a video-game and Internet culture, well-developed, interactive online simulations can stimulate highly effective and engaging learning (Wieman and Perkins, 2006). However, design features of online simulations vary, and can affect results. Critical components of effective online simulations include interactive animations that provide direct responses to users, inviting environment and graphics, simple controls, and real-world connections (Wieman and Perkins, 2006). If used skillfully by the instructor, simulations can push students beyond simply memorizing facts, and encourage using data to support explanations and provide evidence for conclusions (Laxman and Chin, 2011). Research into efficacy of non-traditional labs (online simulations and remote labs) demonstrates that, in at least some regards, non-traditional labs are equally or more effective than traditional hands-on labs. Of 49 studies, 44 showed equal or more effectiveness of non-traditional labs in generating knowledge and understanding (Brinson and Brinson, 2014).

NANSLO began operations in 2011, but there is already some data that supports its effectiveness in online science learning. Students who engaged in NANSLO lab activities while taking online Biology 101 courses through the Colorado Community College System raised their final grade by 10% (Edwards, Mattoon and McKay, 2015). Instructors are strongly encouraged to complete activities themselves before assigning tasks to students, and NANSLO offers guidance to faculty on how best to prepare their students for the lab activities. Advance preparation by faculty is essential to anticipate student problems and questions and leads to increased student engagement. Students in classes that required advance preparation for NANSLO labs reported increased enjoyment and learning from the lab activities (Edwards, Mattoon and McKay, 2015). As with any instructional practice, the pedagogical/andragogical skill and preparation by the instructor affects the success of implementation of NANSLO labs.

5.7 Faculty Liability

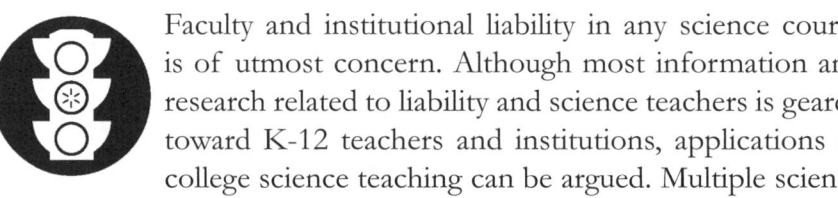 Faculty and institutional liability in any science course is of utmost concern. Although most information and research related to liability and science teachers is geared toward K-12 teachers and institutions, applications to college science teaching can be argued. Multiple science teachers have been sued in the past because of student injuries from experiments that did not go as planned, even because of the student misusing equipment (Nigro, 1988). Without the ability to supervise students completing laboratory investigations in an online class, how can we, as instructors, reduce the risk of student injury? How can we reduce the risk of being sued by students who are completing experiments off campus, without supervision?

Mitigating liability is all about managing risk, whether the class is face-to-face or online. Nothing can eliminate all risk (Nigro, 1988), but there are actions that can reduce the risk. Instructors should always stress lab safety, even though students are using lesser amounts of chemicals and/or household chemicals. You should train students in laboratory safety, and keep a record of that training to create a record that can be used in court to demonstrate that you took precautions to promote safe learning (Love, 2013). You should carefully go through and perform each experiment to look for potential hazards, regardless of whether you wrote the experiment to be completed at home with everyday materials, or a company wrote and supplied lab materials. Consider what mistakes a student might make while performing the experiment and take steps to reduce the chance that students will make that mistake. Teachers should also give instruction to the students over any laboratory activity before asking students to perform that activity. In an online course, this could mean a pre-lab activity, video demonstration, and/or a discussion of potential risks.

Choosing to use a lab kit company could transfer risk liability from the college and instructor to the lab kit company, depending on the company and the contract between the company and the college. However, risk transfer is not a defense in 100% of cases (Love, 2013), and does not eliminate the need for the instructor to go through and perform every lab to ensure student safety and give instruction about the lab and safety issues.

Obviously, the safest option for online courses is using virtual or remote laboratory activities, since they avoid risk inherent in performing laboratory activities at home. However, you must decide if there is an online platform for experiment simulations that fully meets the needs of your course and your students. Even if using all virtual laboratory activities, instructors must still include safety information in their courses, so that students understand risks involved in performing real experiments and learn proper procedures for the future.

Finally, check with your college to determine what type of liability insurance it has and what it covers. Consider purchasing liability insurance through an educator's association; it could help you in the event of criminal charges or civil litigation. The cost of insurance is low when compared to legal fees and other costs associated with a lawsuit (Love, 2013).

SECTION II: BUILDING THE COURSE

CHAPTER 6
MAKING THE MOST OF YOUR LEARNING MANAGEMENT SYSTEM

6.1 Learning Management System Tools

The learning management system (LMS) is the platform you'll use for hosting your course online. There are several LMS options, and different colleges will use different ones. I have used Canvas, Blackboard, and Desire2Learn (Brightspace). They are not all created equal, and each will have features that others don't. Each LMS will have a way to post content, assignments, and quizzes/tests for students. You can also assign due dates, dates for items to be available to students, and more specific restrictions on item availability. The procedures for posting content on each LMS will differ. Refer to your LMS support tutorials for how to post content, assign due dates, and open and close content. Some common tools found in learning management systems are described here.

Announcements

Your LMS will have a main menu and a page where students land first in the course shell. This will likely be the Announcements page, so that students will see any updates you post there when they log into the LMS. In online classes, the LMS course landing page and announcements are often the first items your students will see in your course. You'll want your students' first impression of your course to be welcoming, friendly, and optimistic. You'll also want that first impression to tell students exactly what to do to get started in the course, so that the students will feel comfortable. The first time students log into the course, they will need to know where to go and what to do next, so a good Welcome Announcement can help with that.

Figure 6.1A – Sample Welcome Announcement

Welcome to Online Biology!

If you have any questions as you work through the course, please contact me. Email is the easiest way, and if it's **urgent**, please state that in the subject line of your email. Here is my email address: (include email address), and you can find out more about me by clicking on the "Instructor Information" button on the left side of the screen.

> Include contact information, and how students can find out more about you.

This section is an ONLINE class, which means that you won't have to physically come to class. Sounds great! BUT, you will have class work, labs, and other assignments due each week. **Please scroll down to see all information.**

> A note to scroll down ensures they will see everything.

Here's where you need to start:

> Tell students what to do next.

1. The first thing you'll need to do is read the entire syllabus. Yes, I know you have read lots of them before. Please read it anyway. You can find it under the "Syllabus & Calendar" button on the left side of the screen.
2. Once you have read the syllabus, you can begin working through the course material. Click on the "Units of Study" button on the left side of the screen and begin working in the Unit 1, Week 1, material.

> Show students how to access everything.

Click on the video below to see where things are located in the course and how to access them.

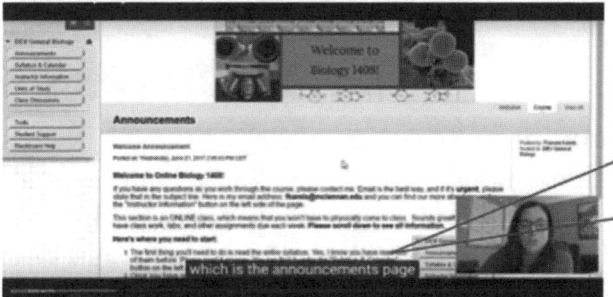

> Screencast video shows how to navigate the course. It was uploaded to YouTube, so I could add Closed-Captioning, and embed it in my LMS course.

In your Welcome Announcement, reassure students that they are in the right place, and let them know you are glad to have them in class. You can introduce yourself as well, but that can make the Welcome Announcement a little long, so I recommend including that information under "Instructor Information." Include a short screencast video that shows students where to find things in the course, including the syllabus.

Use the Announcement tool to incorporate first Principle of Good Practice (Chickering and Gamson, 1987), and initiate contact between you and your students. Email an announcement to students. You can also send a "Remind" (www.remind.com) text message to tell students to read the announcements.

Figure 6.1B – Sample Instructor Information

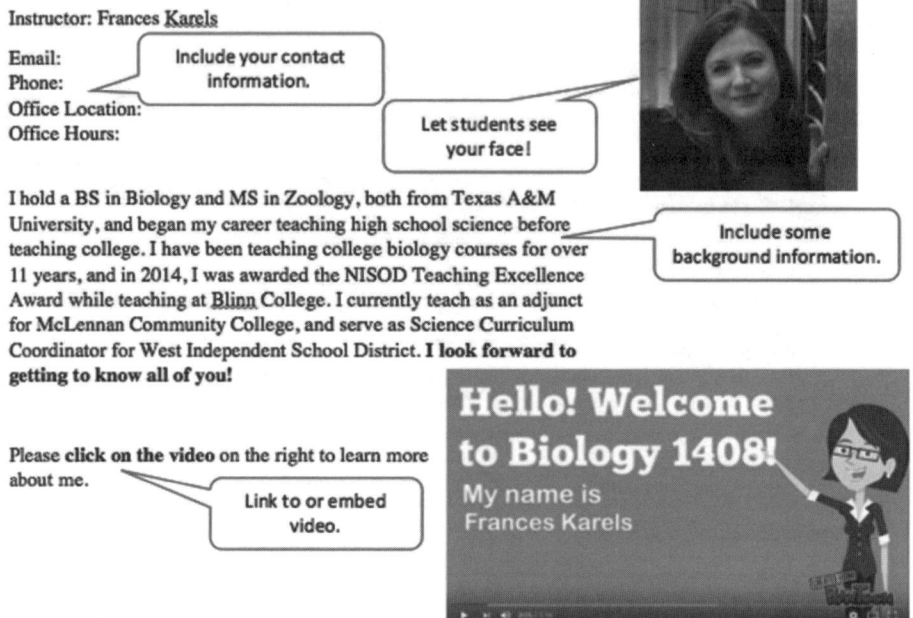

Instructor Information

Include information about yourself, your contact information, office hours, office location, and your average response time to return messages also supports contact between instructor and students, the first Principle of Good Practice (Chickering and Gamson, 1987). You should include a picture and some personal information to allow students to get to know you. I include a Powtoon video with some personal information to spice things up a bit, and a screenshot of it, as well. There is no narration in the video, which is why you won't see an option for closed captioning.

Assignments

Each LMS will offer different assignment options. Typically, you can have quizzes and tests, with several options for question types. Other assignments are submitted through dropboxes, where students upload files. Be sure to tell students what file types you'll accept, since not every file type is compatible with multiple computer systems. In any class, you must include detailed instructions for every assignment, so students know how to complete the assignment. In an online class, you also must ensure students know how each assignment will be graded, and what to expect from each assignment. For example, if you assign a quiz, let students know how many questions there will be, how much time they will have to take the quiz, how it will be graded, and how many attempts they will have. This will take more time up front, but will lead to fewer questions from students later.

Discussions

If you have discussions in your course, students will need to access them frequently. Include a link to each discussion in its appropriate week folder. I recommend also having a main navigation button or tab for discussions so students can access them directly. This will allow students to go directly to a discussion to read and reply rather than having to go through folders to find the discussion every day that they need to post. You might consider having a discussion that stays open the entire course. The name varies (water cooler, off-topic, FAQ discussion), but it is a forum for students to connect just as they would before or after a face-to-face class.

Gradebook

Make sure your gradebook is correctly set up in the LMS so that students will always know their current average in the course. You'll also want to develop a system of naming assignments in the gradebook so that students know which column corresponds to each assignment. One issue you'll need to overcome is that the names of assignments could be cut off in some views of the gradebook, so if you use similar long titles (Unit 1 Assignment 1, Unit 1 Assignment 2), all you or students might see is "Unit 1 A". You can create a shortened version of the assignment name for use in the gradebook, and then let students know where to find that assignment grade in the gradebook. "Unit 1 Assignment 1" could become "U1A1" in the gradebook. "Unit 1 Quiz 1" could become "U1Q1," etc... I prefer to use more descriptive names for assignments, so my gradebook names are based on those.

6.2 Accessibility

In 2013, a student with a visual impairment filed a complaint against the University of Montana. He claimed he could not do his homework because the program was not ADA accessible (Ingeno). Instructors must be concerned with accessibility and there are some special concerns for online courses. The Americans with Disabilities Act prevents colleges from excluding disabled students from accessing technology and programs, even if the courses, technology, or programs are online. However, there are no clear distinctions between what is discriminatory in online education, and what is not. Strive to make your course as accessible as possible, following principles of Universal Design for Learning.

Universal Design

To avoid complaints and discrimination allegations, build your courses to be as accessible to everyone as possible. How? Unfortunately, there's not one set of rules that covers every situation, but there are guidelines for common accessibility issues. Universal Design aims to create an environment (an online class in our case) that is accessible, understandable, and usable by everyone, regardless of disability (National Disability Authority, What Is Universal Design). Universal Design involves two basic ideas: user-aware design and customizable design. User-aware design seeks to create an environment that is inclusive to as many people as possible. Customizable design seeks to create an environment that is adaptable to users with disabilities (National Disability Authority, Definition and Overview). These ideas have been applied to education to create a Universal Design for Learning, which aims to create curriculum that provides everyone an equal opportunity to learn (What Is UDL?).

Universal Design for Learning is guided by three principles:

- Provide Multiple Means of Representation – Students show differences in how they understand material, resulting from physical disabilities, learning disabilities, or learning styles. There is not one way of presenting material that works best for everyone (The Three Principles of UDL), which is why I have advocated so strongly for utilizing multiple types of activities and instructional strategies in your course.

- Provide Multiple Means of Action and Expression – Different students express themselves better through different methods. There is no one method of expression that will work best for all students. In addition, adults like having control of their learning, so choice in expression is desirable.

- Provide Multiple Means of Engagement – Many things affect how each student becomes engaged and motivated to learn, so there is no one method of engagement that works best for all of them. Again, providing multiple types of activities and instructional strategies is vital to creating a successful online course.

Accessibility in online classes requires special attention. For example, it might be tempting to use all sorts of pretty colors and/or fonts when customizing your course shell in the LMS and when typing information for students. I saw an art instructor's course shell, and he had lots of colors to highlight different things, and for artistic design. Here's the problem: some of his students would not be able to read the information well because of visual impairments like color blindness. Any color combinations you use should have enough contrast that a color-blind person can still read the information (Burgstahler, 2017). I stick with basic black fonts. Breaking up the text into paragraphs with white space in between also makes text easier to read online.

Any time you link to something, describe where the link will take the student rather than just writing "click here". This is important for visually impaired students who use screen readers, since only having "click here" is not enough information. Images present another problem for visually impaired students, since there is no way for them to see the image. However, you can add alternative-text (alt-text) with each image, so that a screen reader will read the text describing the image. If the image is not necessary for a visually impaired student (like a picture of where to find a button on the computer screen), you can use "null" as the description, and a screen reader will ignore the image.

Finally, you'll probably have videos in your course. To meet ADA requirements, all videos must have closed captions (Burgstahler, 2017). A transcript is no longer acceptable. Here's the good news: many YouTube videos are already closed-captioned, and you can upload your own videos to YouTube and caption them there before embedding them into your course. If you are just using audio files (no video), a transcript is sufficient.

As I have said before, use consistent organization throughout all aspects of your course. This will allow all students to find everything easier. There may be other issues that arise, so you should contact your college's ADA office to ask questions and determine the expectations for your online course. Once you know the expectations, refer to your college's instructional designer or teaching and learning department for assistance.

Tips for Teaching an Accessible Online Course
Adapted from Disabilities, Opportunities, Internetworking, and Technology (DO-IT), University of Washington

For course web pages, documents, images, and videos
- Use clear, consistent layouts and organization schemes for presenting content.

- Structure headings (using style features built into the Learning Management System, Word, PowerPoint (PPT), PDFs, etc.) and use built-in designs/layouts (e.g., for PPT slides).

- Use descriptive wording for hyperlink text (e.g., "DO-IT Knowledge Base" rather than "click here").

- Minimize the use of PDFs, especially presented when as an image; make sure the text is accessible by testing to see if you can copy and paste it.) Always offer a text based alternative as well.

- Provide concise alternative text descriptions of content presented within images.

- Use large, bold fonts on uncluttered pages with plain backgrounds.

- Use color combinations that are high contrast and can be read by those who are colorblind.

- Make sure all content and navigation is accessible using the keyboard alone.

- Caption or transcribe video and audio content.

With respect to instructional methods

- Assume students have a wide range of technology skills and provide options for gaining the technology skills needed for course participation.

- Present content in multiple ways (e.g., in a combination of text, video, audio, and/or image format).

- Address a wide range of language skills as you write content (e.g., spell acronyms, define terms, avoid or define jargon).

- Make instructions and expectations clear for activities, projects, and assigned reading.

- Make examples and assignments relevant to learners with a wide variety of interests and backgrounds.

- Offer outlines and other scaffolding tools to help students learn.

- Provide adequate opportunities for practice.

- Allow adequate time for activities, projects, and tests (e.g., give details of project assignments in the syllabus so that students can start working on them early).

- Provide feedback on project parts and offer corrective opportunities.

- Provide options for communicating and collaborating that are accessible to individuals with a variety of disabilities.

- Provide options for demonstrating learning (e.g., different types of test items, portfolios, presentations, discussions).

CHAPTER 7
LESSON DESIGN FOR ONLINE DELIVERY

Don't worry. This chapter is not about designing technology or software. It's about determining which lessons you already use can be restructured for online delivery and maximizing the efficacy of lessons you use in your online class. A benefit of designing an online course is that you will be able to carefully analyze your current lessons and ensure that they are as engaging and effective as possible.

You're probably comfortable planning a course for face-to-face delivery, and the good news is that much of that planning translates well to online delivery. (If you're new to teaching and have never planned a face-to-face course, visit the Part-Time Press [Part-timePress.com] for excellent resources.) You will still need to carefully plan your course, outline the semester and assign due dates, develop instructions for activities and assignments, and build lessons. You'll also have to devise strategies to retain your online students and help them succeed.

7.1 Student Learning Objectives

We should all have student learning outcomes and/or objectives for our courses. The Sixth Principle of Good Practice emphasizes holding high expectations (Chickering and Gamson, 1987), and learning objectives convey those high expectations to your students. Learning objectives may be provided/required by the state or your college, or you may write your own. Learning objectives help instructors focus on the material students need to learn, and help students know what material to focus on in their classes. Adult learners, especially in an online course, need to be aware of how the activities they complete relate to learning objectives. When students understand how what they do in the course assists in their learning of the material, lessons go more smoothly.

Have high expectations, and ensure all course and lesson learning objectives are measurable.

If you have course objectives provided for you, look them over to see that they are measurable. Stating that a student should understand something is not measurable, since students may think they understand something when they don't. Providing measurable objectives allows students to better track their mastery of course material. There are several resources available to help you with this. When I write learning objectives, I like to use a list of verbs classified according to their level of complexity according to revised Bloom's Taxonomy.

Bloom's Taxonomy, originally published in 1956 by lead author Benjamin Bloom, attempted to classify types of thinking from simple to more complex. That taxonomy was revised in 2001 by Lorin Anderson, a former student of Bloom, and David Krathwohl, who worked with Bloom on the original publication. Revised Bloom's Taxonomy renamed some components, used verbs instead of nouns, and switched the order of synthesis and evaluation in the original Bloom's taxonomy, to evaluating and creating (Wilson, 2013). Both the original and revised taxonomy schemes classify learning activities based on their level of complexity.

Figure 7.1A: Bloom's Taxonomy (Revised)

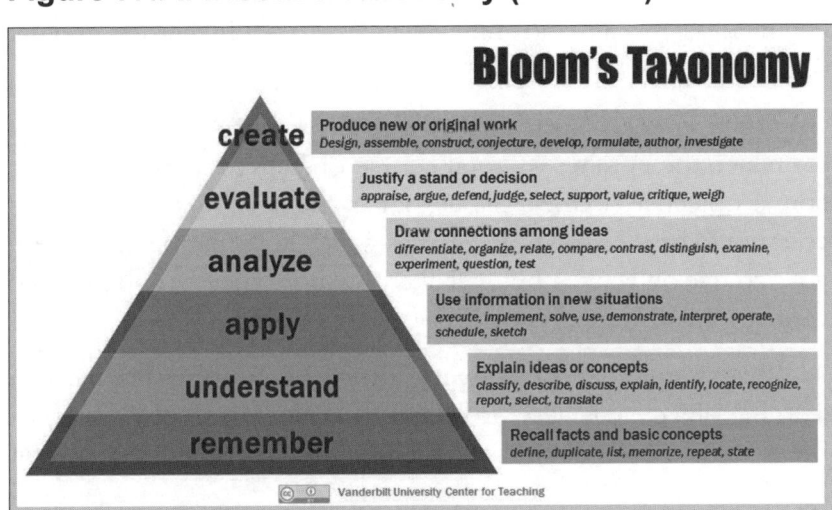

In college science courses, you must have high expectations for your students, and write learning objectives based on the higher levels of Bloom's Taxonomy. Students may still need to progress through lower level activities to obtain the knowledge needed for the higher-level activities, but instructors should expect students to progress to higher-level activities, especially in majors' science courses. Keep this in mind as you write objectives for your online course. Figure 7.1A on the previous page from the Vanderbilt University Center for Teaching outlines the levels of the revised Bloom's Taxonomy, and includes some verbs to accompany each level.

 An Internet search for Revised Bloom's Taxonomy Verbs will return many sources with verbs like the one above. That will allow you to select verbs based on the activities students are doing, and identify the level of cognition required by the task.

Here's an example from biology for non-science majors: *"In this class, students learn about the cell cycle, mitosis, and meiosis."* While this statement is true, it is not a good learning objective. It is too broad, and not measurable. Instead, use verbs based in revised Bloom's Taxonomy: "Students will be able to *identify* stages of the cell cycle, mitosis, and meiosis in plant and animal cells." That statement is measurable, but is only written at the "understand" level of Bloom's taxonomy. To increase the complexity, the objective could be revised. "Students will be able to *demonstrate* stages of the cell cycle, mitosis, and meiosis, in plant and animal cells." This is a higher-level course objective.

Often, course objectives are written in very vague or broad terms to reduce the number of total course objectives. You'll post your course objectives in the syllabus, but as you develop online lessons, you should have lesson objectives as well. These may be the same as your course objectives, but will likely be more specific and progress through the lower levels of Bloom's Taxonomy.

Take the course objective written above, for example. The learning objective is very broad, so to create lesson objectives, we break it into parts (chunking). What is the first thing students will learn? From the previous objective, we first cover interphase, since it includes stages common to mitosis and meiosis. For this first lesson on the cell cycle, we need a learning objective more tailored to that lesson. By the end of the lesson on interphase, students will be able to demonstrate the stages of interphase, including G1, S, and G2. Notice I left out any mention of mitosis and meiosis. They will come later.

 Chunk your online lessons into smaller parts that are easier for students to complete at one time. Some students may work in the online class for a couple of hours two or three times a week, while others will work in shorter, more frequent periods. Breaking up your lessons into smaller parts accommodates each type of student.

7.2 Creating Diverse Learning Experiences

After you have written measurable course objectives, you'll begin thinking about what activities would be most appropriate to help students master those objectives. You probably know what content you want to teach, but the "how" in your online course will likely be different than in your face-to-face courses. Why? Besides the different format, you could also have different demographics in the student population of your online course. Respecting the diverse talents and ways of learning of your students is the last of the Seven Principles of Good Practice (Chickering and Gamson, 1987). Students come into your class with different experiences (the first adult learning principle), which affect how they process information (Conaway and Zorn-Arnold, 2015).

Research the demographics of your college's online students to better prepare your course for those types of learners.

In 2011, almost seven million, approximately 32 percent of total students, took at least one online course (Allen and Seaman, 2013). Thirty-eight percent of all undergraduates were over the age of 25, and by 2019, that percent is expected to reach almost 50 percent (Hess, 2011). Online students often have nontraditional characteristics. These characteristics include having independent status, having children, having a GED, attending college more than one year after high school graduation, attending only part-time, and working full-time. Many of your students will have at least one of these characteristics, and it is likely that some will have more than one (Radford, Cominole and Skomsvold, 2015). The table below summarizes nontraditional characteristics data from online students in 2011-12.

Figure 7.2A – Characteristics of Students Who Took Some or All of Their Courses Online

Nontraditional Characteristic	Some Online Classes	All Online Classes	Entire Program Online
Independent Status	25.4%	12.4%	10.1%
Has Dependents	25.8%	15.2%	12.4%
Single with Dependents	25.5%	12.4%	10.6%
GED or Other Certificate	22.9%	9.9%	8.0%
More Than One Year Since High School Graduation	23.5%	11.7%	9.7%
Part-time Status	25.7%	9.6%	6.9%
Worked Full-time	26.8%	15.7%	12.8%

Adapted from Demographic and Enrollment Characteristics of Nontraditional Undergraduates: 2011–12 (Radford, Cominole and Skomsvold, 2015).

Figure 7.2B – Percentage of Students with One, Two, Three, or Four Nontraditional Characteristics Taking Some or All Courses Online

Number of Nontraditional Characteristics	Some Classes Online	All Classes Online	Entire Degree Program Online
One	24.3%	4.9%	3.4%
Two - Three	24.6%	9.8%	7.7%
Four or More	25.9%	15.1%	12.4%

Adapted from Demographic and Enrollment Characteristics of Nontraditional Undergraduates: 2011–12 (Radford, Cominole and Skomsvold, 2015).

As you plan your course, consider the characteristics of your future students. You may already know what types of students you typically see in your face-to-face classes, but they may differ in your online classes. When you design your online course, recognize that the students in your courses will have different learning preferences and backgrounds, and diversify your instructional strategies to better meet the needs of your diverse students (Leonard, 2000).

Dale's Cone of Experience lists distinct types of experiences, from more abstract (top of the Cone) to more concrete applications (bottom of the Cone). Dale argued that instructors should include instructional strategies that directly and physically engage students in learning activities, in addition to the more abstract learning experiences such as reading or listening to lecture (Dale, 1970). On the following page, I have included a diagram of Dale's Cone of Experience, along with updated information about what types of activities could be implemented at each level.

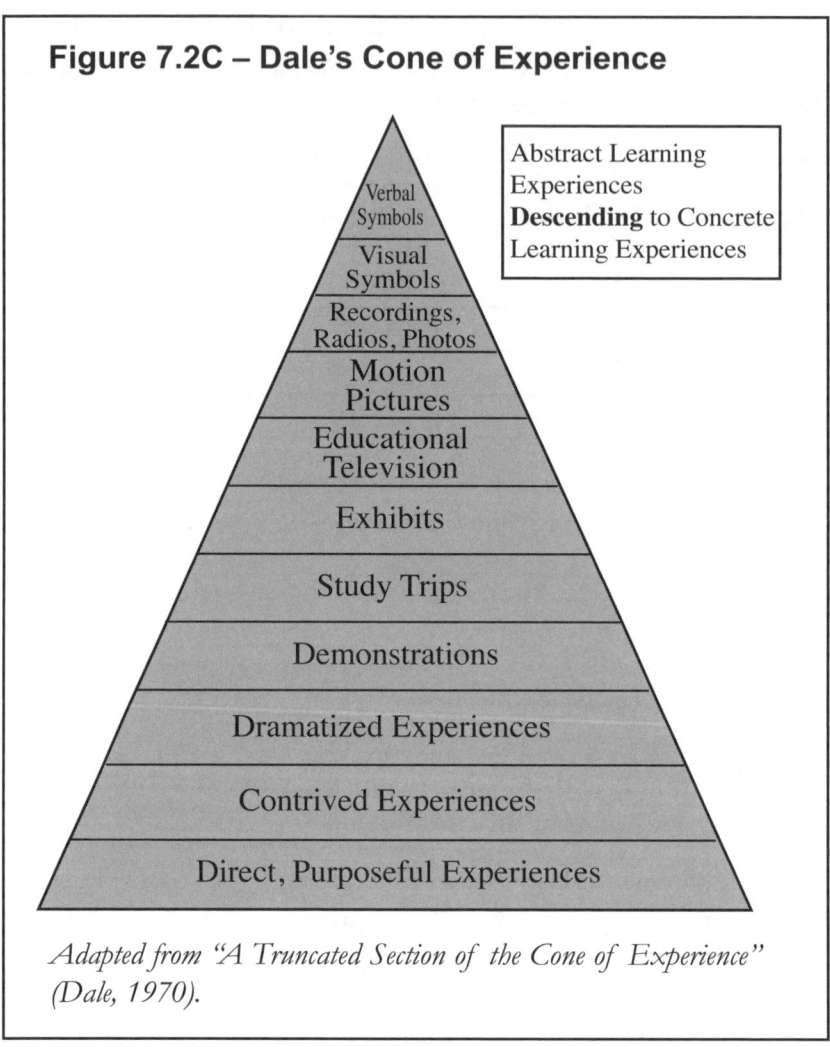

Figure 7.2C – Dale's Cone of Experience

Abstract Learning Experiences **Descending** to Concrete Learning Experiences

Verbal Symbols
Visual Symbols
Recordings, Radios, Photos
Motion Pictures
Educational Television
Exhibits
Study Trips
Demonstrations
Dramatized Experiences
Contrived Experiences
Direct, Purposeful Experiences

Adapted from "A Truncated Section of the Cone of Experience" (Dale, 1970).

These are the levels of Dale's Cone of Experience, and some examples of how those types of activities might be used in an online science course.

Verbal symbols: Dale called these the "pinnacle of the Cone." They are the most abstract (Dale, 1970). Try to build a course without any words, however, and you'll find it is extremely difficult; furthermore, Dale did not advocate this. Dale's research suggests that visual symbols should accompany other types of experiences.

Visual symbols: Dale included chalkboard communication, flat maps, diagrams, and charts in this category. In science, maps, diagrams, and charts are extremely valuable when discussing certain topics (Dale, 1970). Geology uses maps extensively. Diagrams are useful in all aspects of science for describing processes, locations, physical structures, etc. Charts help us summarize data so that trends can better be visualized.

Photos, realistic drawings, radio, and recordings: These contain aspects of videos, but not all of the aspects together. However, images are more readily available due to the Internet, and images are available online for use under Creative Commons Licenses. Radio and recordings are of use to us as online instructors, since we can make our own recordings to pass along specialized information to our students.

Television and motion pictures: We would probably lump these together now under a section titled "video." There are so many more options today than Dale could have imagined. YouTube is a wonderful example, with its collection of short videos on a multitude of subjects. Dale noted the value of film and television for their realistic, organized, clear, and dramatic expression of ideas (Dale, 1970), and this still holds true today.

Exhibits: Dale refers to two kinds of exhibits: those that students observe, and those that students produce themselves. What the two kinds of exhibits have in common is that both will be observed by someone (Dale, 1970). Students could observe exhibits from art galleries or museums, or produce an exhibit over a topic as a project for other students to observe. In an online science class, it could be difficult to find a single type of exhibit that all students would be able to attend. However, you could still require students to create their own exhibits as a project.

Study trips: Study trips take students outside the classroom setting, and are commonly called field trips or field work now. Classes may go to a museum, zoo, or aquarium. Students may be asked to go to a location to make observations, collect data, or participate in citizen science projects. In online classes, the class would not go together, but students could travel somewhere near their location to complete a task or assignment. For example, I have a Nature Selfie assignment in which students travel to a park or other natural area and take a picture of the ecosystem. Then students analyze the levels of biological organization of the ecosystem as well as the taxonomy of one of the organisms. The requirement of a park or natural area is vague enough that students can find a place near them that would meet the requirement.

Demonstration: A demonstration is an active, visual representation of an idea or process. In science, instructors often demonstrate proper use of lab equipment or procedures.

Dramatization: A dramatization includes acting or watching others act to illustrate a point or demonstrate a process. This might not be as common in science classes as in other classes. For any kind of historical event, however, dramatization could have enormous potential. Students could watch a dramatization, or actually participate.

Contrived Experience: A contrived experience involves models or other representations of concepts, like simulations or virtual labs, that allow students to observe or interact with things that would otherwise be impossible. For example, we cannot directly observe how the continents have drifted over time, but using the EarthViewer app from Howard Hughes Medical Institute (http://www.hhmi.org/biointeractive/earthviewer), students can still visualize the process.

Direct, Purposeful Experience: Direct, purposeful experiences immerse students in hands-on learning. For science, this would include laboratory activities in which students are actively engaged in performing experiments.

 Dale's Cone of Experience has sometimes been credited as the basis for the Pyramid of Learning, which suggests learning retention is higher with some instructional strategies than with others. However, there is evidence that suggests students can learn and retain information from activities on all levels of the pyramid (Lalley and Miller, 2007). Dale stated explicitly that the narrowing of the Cone at the top does not correlate to difficulty of learning from those activities, and was

careful to remind his readers not to take the Cone literally. He presented his Cone as a reminder of the options available for learning activities in classes, and urged teachers to "make effective use of a purposeful mixture of all these educative possibilities" (Dale, 1970). When planning your online course, integrate multiple instructional strategies so learners have the most opportunities to be successful.

Perhaps it is time to reorganize Dale's Cone of Experience, so that we can see each aspect of learning as integral parts of the whole process. We can look at it like a like the diagram below, with sections interconnected and labeled with updated versions of Dale's Cone labels. I have changed Verbal Symbols to Written Words/Text, and combined Visual Symbols and Still Pictures together into a section called Images. Radio and Recordings become Audio, Motion Pictures and Educational Television together become Video. For online science classes, Exhibits are labeled as Projects, and Study Trips can be labeled as Field Work or Field Trips. Contrived experiences are perhaps more common now in the age of computer simulations, and in science we often use computer models or simulations. To better fit online science classes, Contrived Experiences is relabeled as Simulations and Virtual Lab Activities.

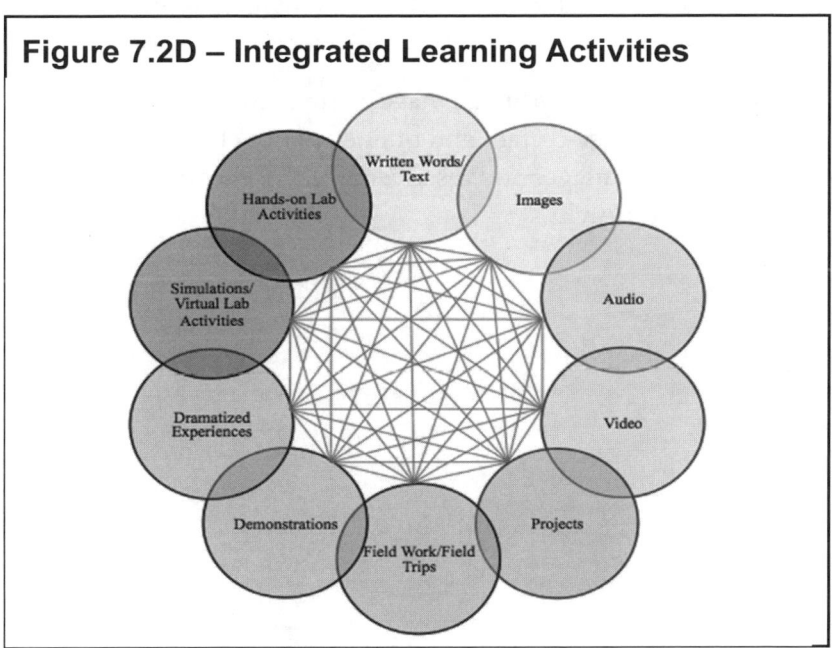

Figure 7.2D – Integrated Learning Activities

I'm not suggesting the makeup of your class include every type of learning activity equally. For example, in a science course in which 50 percent of the time is spent on laboratory activities, it could be difficult to ensure that all types of learning activities have equal presence in a classroom. However, there are still other types of learning experiences integrated into the lab activities. You will probably have instructions that students read (text) that also include some pictures or diagrams (images). You might even include a short video to demonstrate a certain procedure. That same lab activity may integrate a model, like a virtual lab. Another type of laboratory would include hands-on activities. What you might not have in your online course are field trips and dramatized experiences. Be creative, however, and you might find a way to work that in as well.

Dale's point, and mine, is that we should all strive to incorporate multiple types of learning activities in our courses. Some types of learning activities may be more prevalent than others. In fact, Hands-on Lab Activities would be a larger piece of the graph in laboratory courses than in other types of courses. So, in online science courses with a lab component, a graph of proportional time devoted to several types of learning activities would show Hand-on Lab Activities, Simulations/Virtual Lab Activities, Written Words/Text, and Demonstrations as more prevalent in the class.

On the following pages, I have compared types of learning activities used in face-to-face and online science class lesson design, outlining the advantages and disadvantages of each type of course design tool and activity.

Learning Activities in Online/F2F Science Courses

Face-to-Face Activities	Online Alternatives
Lecture Advantages: • Students can ask questions in real time • Can lead to class discussion Disadvantages: • Passive learning • Minimal engagement	**Recorded Lecture** Advantages: • Students can start and stop recording at their own pace and on their own time. • Students can listen to lecture more than once. Disadvantages: • Passive learning • Minimal engagement **Video/Animations** Advantages: • Students can start and stop recordings at their own pace and on their own time. • Students can view more than once. • As an alternative to lecture, can be more engaging due to rich graphics and production values. Disadvantages: • Copyright concerns • Passive learning

Learning Activities in Online/F2F Science Courses

Face-to-Face Activities	Online Alternatives
Reading Textbook	**Reading Textbook**

Reading Textbook

Advantages:

- Students obtain information.

Disadvantages:

- Passive Learning

- Not Engaging

- Poor readers may have trouble comprehending information.

Reading Textbook

Advantages:

- Students obtain information

Disadvantages:

- Passive Learning

- Not Engaging

- Poor readers may have trouble comprehending information.

Online Homework System (Used as homework)

Advantages:

- Students interact with textbook material.

1. Students can complete assignments to check comprehension of lesson.

Disadvantages:

- Often requires a subscription fee paid by the student.

- Students could be confused about completion dates.

- Students may not fully understand material and receive low grades on homework.

Online Homework System (Used as part of learning process)

Advantages:

- Students interact with textbook material.

1. Students can complete tutorial activities to gain knowledge.

2. Tutorial activities help students who have trouble comprehending the text.

Disadvantages:

- Often requires a subscription fee paid by the student.

- Students could be confused about which items they should complete when.

Learning Activities in Online/F2F Science Courses

Face-to-Face Activities	Online Alternatives
Hands-on Laboratory Activities Advantages: • Engaging • Active learning • Real world application • Authentic learning Disadvantages: • Safety risks • Require specialized equipment • Require specialized chemicals	**Lab Kits** Advantages: • Engaging • Active learning • Real world application • Authentic learning • Pre-packaged • Students order from company or campus bookstore • Reduced liability compared to labs using household materials Disadvantages: • Safety risk • Less flexibility – must use labs designed by company • Students may not order and/or receive kits on time • Increased cost to student **Labs Using Household Materials** Advantages: • Engaging • Active Learning

Learning Activities in Online/F2F Science Courses

Face-to-Face Activities	Online Alternatives
	• More design flexibility
	Disadvantages:
	• Equipment and supply constraints
	• Safety Risk
	• Liability
	Virtual Labs Advantages:
	• Engaging
	• Active learning
	• Real world application
	• Authentic learning
	• Reduced safety risk
	• Reduced liability
	• Can simulate long-term experiments
	• Can simulate experiments in different geographic locations
	Disadvantages:
	• Not Hands-On
	• Can't replicate every experiment

Learning Activities in Online/F2F Science Courses

Face-to-Face Activities	Online Alternatives
	NANSLO Advantages: • Engaging • Active learning • Real world application • Authentic learning • Reduced safety risk • Reduced liability • Can work with NANSLO lab techs • NANSLO experiments are open source. Disadvantages: • Experiment constraints • Equipment constraints • Instructors must book time for students. • Students must schedule experiments within windows of time.
Quizzes/Tests Advantages: • Summative assessment data • Easy to schedule during class time	**Quizzes/Tests** Advantages: • Summative assessment data • Computer can grade most questions

Learning Activities in Online/F2F Science Courses

Face-to-Face Activities	Online Alternatives
Disadvantages:	Disadvantages:

Disadvantages:

- Time taken from instruction
- Grading time

Discussions
Advantages:

- Can be spontaneous
- Can be used as formative assessment

Disadvantages:

- Not everyone participates
- Difficult to grade
- No time for students to research responses

Group Collaboration
Advantages:

- Students can physically meet during class and/or outside of class

Disadvantages:

- Not everyone participates and contributes

Disadvantages:

- Potential cost for proctoring

Discussions
Advantages:

- Can be used as formative assessment
- Easier to keep track of who responds
- Asynchronous nature allows students to research information for responses.
- More time for grading and feedback
- Can grade using a rubric

Disadvantages:

- Must be planned in advance
- Students could lurk until others have answered
- Writing responses could take more time for students

Group Collaboration
Advantages:

- Students can meet via the Internet according to their own schedules

Disadvantages:

- Not everyone participates and contributes

Learning Activities in Online/F2F Science Courses

Face-to-Face Activities	Online Alternatives
Written Assignment Advantages: • Can submit on paper or online via the LMS • Instructors can give verbal or written feedback Disadvantages: • Grading Time	**Written Assignment** Advantages: • Can submit on paper online via the LMS • Instructors can give verbal or written feedback • Can use plagiarism detection software Disadvantages: • Grading Time

7.3 Active Learning

Multiple options exist for distributing information to students, yet many instructors rely on lecturing to students and having students read the textbook. These two strategies are not active learning, and should not comprise the majority of lessons in your online course. We discussed issues with students reading the textbook in Chapter 4, so we'll focus on lecture here. Lecture is rarely the best way for students to learn for deep understanding, critical analysis, and application. I'm not saying you'll never need to record information for your students, but you should keep it short. Longer lectures can lead to more mind wandering, which can lead to less information being remembered by students (Risko, et al., 2012).

Since we want students to be able to apply scientific principles and processes, integrating active learning in lesson design is important. To maximize active learning, instructors must maximize student interaction with each other and the course content.

Teaching science online using active learning can be accomplished, if instructors reconsider the methods they use in face-to-face courses, carefully plan in advance and require student interaction in the course as a part of their grades (Miller, 2008).

 Minimize lecture in your online classes. As you design lessons for your online course, always design with your learning objectives in mind. Lecture may be more appropriate for objectives that involve the lower levels of Bloom's Taxonomy: remembering and understanding. Since lecture can activate short-term memory (Johnson and Barrett, 2017; McLaughlin and Mandin, 2001), if you lecture, help students develop note-taking skills to assist in the transfer of information from short-term to long-term memory. Also, you should consider your presentation of the material, since that likely affects student attention (Wilson and Korn, 2007).

We've all been trapped in a lecture that was, for whatever reason, painful for the listener. Lecturalgia, as described by McLaughlin and Mandin, can result from poor judgement, poor organization, and/or poor delivery. If you lecture, consider how you portray your subject and the following recommendations as you plan your lecture:

- Aim to enhance knowledge and understanding (McLaughlin and Mandin, 2001). You're telling students information when you lecture, so focus on activities to enhance higher-level learning.

- Be knowledgeable and interested in the subject. Your students will be listening to you, so lecture is your chance to show your interest and personality. If you're bored by the information, your students will be as well.

- Be aware of prior knowledge and needs of audience. Acknowledge that some of your students will have more prior knowledge than others. Some will need more reference information than others. Keep your lecture short and focused, but suggest other resources if students need more information.

- Provide objectives and identify key points. Make a point to tell students what you will be covering and how it relates to other activities. Identifying key points will help students learn to take notes over lecture information, and convert the information to long-term memory.

- Align and limit content to the objectives. I took an online graduate course in which the instructor lectured for at least an hour over each chapter. He would start discussing something, and then would say, "But that's just FYI." It was difficult to know what was just "FYI" and what I should know. Students want to know what they need to learn to do well in the course. Your course objectives should help them with this, so keep your information focused on the objectives.

- Use illustrations and examples. Most instructors take advantage of presentation software to include illustrations. Examples could include case studies or data, or samples of student work if you are discussing assignment instructions.

- Plan to facilitate learning after the lecture. Students need to do something with the information you present in lecture. It should lead somewhere, like to an activity in which students will apply the information. Application of knowledge is often a more essential skill than memorization (Johnson and Barrett, 2017), especially in science.

If you choose to lecture, follow the recommendations above to make your lectures as engaging as possible. In addition, upload the files you use during the lecture, so students have a template for taking notes. Consider the file types you upload, though. For example, many textbook publishers provide PowerPoint template files for instructors to modify and use during lecture. You'll probably find that some students do not have access to Microsoft software, because they use a free version like Open Office, or use a Mac. You can export the file into a .pdf format, or try some other options. There are so many other forms of presentation software you can use. Here are just a few:

Powtoon – Powtoon (www.Powtoon.com) is an online presentation platform that is an alternative to PowerPoint. You can include animated characters, text, pictures, and even create your own avatar by uploading a photo of yourself. It's perfect for introducing yourself to students and going over basic information. There is a paid version, but I have never opted for the paid version. So far, I have been able to do everything I need with the free version. **Assignment example:** students must develop their own presentation on an assigned topic. They could use Powtoon to make the presentation that would then be shared with the class.

Animoto – Animoto (www.Animoto.com) allows you (or your students) to create videos quickly and easily by uploading pictures. The amount of text per slide is limited, however, so Animoto works best for presentations in which you have more pictures.

Assignment example: students must find at least 5 real-world examples of something you have discussed in class. They could take pictures of the items and upload the pictures into an Animoto video, and briefly explain how each picture relates to what has been covered in class. They could submit the link to you in the LMS dropbox or by email, and it could be shared with the class.

OfficeMix – OfficeMix allows you to narrate a PowerPoint presentation, so you can use it to record brief lectures. You or your college must purchase a license for OfficeMix to use it. Check with your college IT department to see if you have access through a site license.

Camtasia – Camtasia is a screencasting tool that also requires a license. A screencasting tool allows you to record what you are doing on your computer screen, along with your audio narration. Again, your college may have a license that would allow you to download and use the software.

Screencast-o-matic (www.screencast-o-matic.com) is a free online screencasting platform. I like it because you can select which portion of the screen to record, rather than just the entire desktop. For the free version, videos are limited to 15 minutes each, but that's more time than I typically use for screencasts.

Screencastify (www.screencastify) is a Google extension that allows you to record your desktop and narration. I like it because I can upload the video directly to my Google Drive, which facilitates easy sharing. It also has some tools that Screencast-o-matic does not.

Research has shown that students demonstrate increased learning when engaged in active learning (LoPresto and Slater, 2016), and the third Principle of Good Practice encourages active learning (Chickering and Gamson, 1987). Active learning engages students with course materials, allowing them to apply information, rather than simply listening or memorizing information (Harvard University). Students participating in active learning activities perform better when applying material (Johnson and Barrett, 2017).

Active learning involves authenticity, which can be defined in slightly different ways. Educators refer to authenticity as learning that applies information in the same manner as in the real world. For students, however, authenticity relates to relevancy to their lives (Egbert and Roe, 2014). In online classes, instructors must pay close attention to authenticity, since students will not be in physical laboratories using laboratory equipment.

The 5E Model

The 5E Instructional Model can be used in science education to increase student interaction with course content (Leonard, 2000). The 5E Model consists of five stages: **Engage**, **Explore**, **Explain**, **Elaborate**, and **Evaluate**. Typically, the 5E Model would comprise a unit of two to three weeks in length (Bybee, 2014), which is applicable to college science courses. Each of the five stages are explained below, with suggestions for application to online science courses.

Engage: Engaging learners involves capturing student attention, sparking interest, activating prior knowledge, and identifying misconceptions (Bybee, et al., 2006). You can do this by presenting students with a problem, asking a question, or presenting situations that seem to defy understanding (Bybee, 2014). In online courses, you could use a news article or video that describes a recent event that relates to information in the unit. A demonstration is engaging as well, since students might be curious about how it was done. For my lesson on the cell cycle, I try to spark student interest in the cell cycle by including a video animation comparing normal cell replication and cancer cell replication, and asking some guiding questions. How does the cell cycle regulate cell division? How can alterations to the cell cycle result in cancer? I include a brief discussion forum, asking students to post topics about which they would like more information. Addressing topics students want to learn, and topics which relate to their future careers meets your adult students' need to know, readiness to learn, and make learning relevant.

Explore: In science courses, exploration often involves laboratory investigations in which students connect prior knowledge to new information (Bybee, et al., 2006). Since each student comes in with a separate set of prior experiences, the connections made will vary for each student. Students in the Explore stage are trying to satisfy the curiosity stimulated during the Engage stage. Introduce Explore activities, provide necessary background information, and provide materials and equipment (Bybee, 2014). In online classes, instructors must ensure students obtain necessary equipment and materials, explain proper use of equipment and materials and provide essential safety warnings. For this stage, I thought about what materials students could purchase and use to make a cell cycle kit. I bought materials and created a short video demonstrating how to put the kit together. I added several animations and diagrams and asked the students to replicate the cell cycle. Students submitted videos of themselves using the materials to simulate the phases of the cell cycle and mitosis, and then later, meiosis. This came closest to what I have students do in face-to-face classes, which is to simulate the cell phases while I watch and ask questions. The goal is not to necessarily have something to grade, but to help students master the material.

Explain: In this stage, the instructor introduces concepts, processes, or skills that build upon the Engage and Explore activities. Students should be given opportunities to demonstrate understanding and/or skills (Bybee, et al., 2006). In online courses, instructors can record short, concise lectures, use video, the Internet, or simulations (Bybee, 2014). In this stage, I include more videos, and an online laboratory activity. In the laboratory activity, students learn to identify stages of the cell cycle in plant cells and animal cells. Students then complete a quiz about the identification of the stages of the cell cycle (immediate feedback). They can also utilize activities from the online homework system for more practice.

Elaborate: In the Elaboration phase, students are challenged to apply what they have learned in new ways. Students are encouraged to interact with each other and the information (Bybee, 2014). The goal is for students to conduct activities to deepen their understanding and develop their skills (Bybee, et al., 2006). A well-planned discussion challenges students to solve a problem using information they have learned, share their ideas and support their positions. In this stage, I challenge my online students to answer the guiding questions from the Engage stage in a discussion forum. In some Learning Management Systems, you can utilize a "post first" feature, which requires that students post an answer before they can view other students' answers. I like to use this feature so that students have to formulate their own answers rather than summarizing what others have written. I ask probing questions, clarify misunderstandings, and keep the discussion moving in a positive direction.

Evaluate: Throughout the learning process (the prior 4 stages), teachers should assess student understanding and skills and provide feedback (Bybee, 2014). Formative assessments can and should be used for this purpose, and we will discuss formative assessments in Chapter 13. In the Evaluate stage, teachers are typically implementing a summative assessment, based on the level of complexity of the teaching, that measures mastery of learning objectives (Bybee, et al., 2006). For a summative evaluation, combine aspects of previous formative assessments. For instance, ask multiple choice questions, have students identify stages of the cell cycle from slide pictures, and/or have them write an essay.

 An active learning strategy often implemented in science education is inquiry-based learning, because it most closely follows steps in the scientific method. The process is learner-centered, and focuses on process, reflection, and self-assessment (Cattaneo, 2017). Students exposed to inquiry-based (guided-inquiry) laboratory activities showed more positive attitudes and less anxiety. The inquiry-based methods were difficult for students at first, since the process was new to them, but at the end of the course, students preferred it over more teacher-directed laboratory activities. Students also showed better learning outcomes from guided-inquiry, and better understood the importance of laboratory steps (Ural, 2016).

7.4 Group Collaboration

The second Principle of Good Practice in Undergraduate Education encourages developing reciprocity and cooperation among students (Chickering and Gamson, 1987). We can facilitate this by requiring students to collaborate in their learning. Group collaboration is often included in active learning activities (Harvard University) because it increases student interaction and encourages students to be active participants in their own learning.

 Include group collaboration opportunities in your course, but design projects so that students will not benefit from loafing.

When collaborating, students need to understand what is expected of each group member, and what roles need to be filled. Faculty members should assign an activity that illustrates types of group roles, and could help students assign roles to members as needed. Group projects need detailed instructions that outline the project goals, essential requirements, and timeline (Morgan, et al., 2014).

It is possible to design a group project that allows for individual grading based on individual contribution to the project. When you design a group project, you'll need to outline roles in the project according to the number of students in each group. For example, you may assign different aspects of the research to each group member, and require each to submit their research to the group by some preliminary deadline. Then, the group would discuss (in an online discussion forum) each member's research, and work together to revise, edit, and compile the research into one unified presentation. If any group member fails to complete their portion of research, then they can be fired from the group and must complete the entire project on their own. This helps ensure that the group members who do not want to work are identified and removed from the group before the actual collaboration begins. I have included an outline of a project I have used for introductory biology.

Figure 7.4A – Virtual Collection Group Project Guidelines

Instructions

Group Project - Virtual Collection Guidelines

Individual Component of Virtual Collection:

Digital photographs of six (6) different species, with appropriate descriptions and information described below.

Checklist of required specimens for **individual** collection:

The six photographs must contain each of the six types of organisms from the taxon list. Among these six specimens from the taxon list, three must meet the specifications on the category list. For example, a fish is both a vertebrate **and** aquatic:

Taxon List:	*Category List:*
Vertebrate	aquatic
Invertebrate	terrestrial
Seed plant	microscopic
Seedless plant	
Fungus	
Protist	

Species Criteria

Must be living at time of photographic collection (i.e., not a dead or dried specimen or shell)

Must be native (i.e., cannot be a planting, a cultivar or introduced species).

Documentation

The list of rules below is meant to ensure that each photograph taken is unique to your collection (i.e. not pulled from the Internet, a magazine, a friend, etc.)

- For stationary organisms, the photograph must include your ID as proof of individual collection. This means you must place your ID in the frame of the photograph before taking the photograph.

- For mobile organisms (birds, mammals, insects, etc.) you must take two photographs. The first should include the organism in its surroundings and the second should include the same frame with your ID in the frame, as verification that you took the photograph (In this second image, the organism may or may not be present).

- The photograph must be clear (i.e., not blurry) and the organism must be clearly identifiable from the image.

Individual Presentation Criteria

You will submit your images to your instructor in a format of your choosing, as long as all required information is included. For each image, include the following information:

- Date, time, state, county, location, temperature, and weather

- Correct classification of the organism to the taxonomic rank of Class (i.e. must include Domain, Kingdom, Phylum, Class). Any other required taxonomic levels will be left to your professor's discretion.

- An overview of the natural history of the organism including a description of the organism, its distribution, and its ecological role in the community (this information will be recorded in the notes section of the slide).

- References must be cited for each specimen (e.g., where did you get your information?) Include in-text citations and a works cited list for each organism/slide.

Timeline

You will turn in one (1) completed slide before spring break to determine if your overall process is correct. See the course schedule and/or your instructor for more due date information.

Group Component of Virtual Collection

In addition to the individual component of the collection, students will form groups and work together to collect additional specimens. The number of additional specimens will be equal to the number of group members. For example, if there are 3 students in your group, your group would have 3 additional specimens.

Checklist of required specimens for group collection

- Taxon List:

- Microscopic specimen (pond water specimen)

- Fungus

- Invertebrate (can be photographed in a collection jar)

- If there are 4 people in your group, your fourth specimen must be a seedless plant.

Group Presentation Criteria

In addition to all criteria for the individual presentations, the group presentation will adhere to the following:

- The group presentation will consist of the group specimens and two (2) specimens from each group member's individual collection. For example, if the group has three members, the group presentation will be composed of three (3) group specimens, and two (2) specimens from member 1, and two (2) specimens from member 2, and two (2) specimens from member 3, for a total of nine (9) total specimens in the collection.

- None of the specimens in the group collection can be duplicates. Each of the specimens must represent a different species.

- The group will give a presentation discussing the group collection.

- Each member will discuss his/her specimens from the individual collection. Each group member should plan to talk from 1 to 2 minutes each about their individual specimens and ONE group specimen. For example, if there are 3 people in the group, each person would discuss one group specimen and their 2 individual specimens. This ensures all group members share in the work and preparation of the project.

Documentation

In addition to all criteria for the individual and group collection, each individual and group must do the following:

- Include in the photograph the ID of each member of the group, or other documentation demonstrating that the image is unique to your group's collection (see documentation of individual collection).

- For the microscopic image, more documentation is required than the other images. Upon collection of a pond water sample, you take a photograph of the collection site while collecting your sample. You will bring your pond water sample to the lab on specified dates to use lab microscopes. Each group will take the microscopic image and immediately present it to your instructor for approval and verification. Additionally, the microscopic image should include a picture of all group members surrounding the microscope while the slide is still on the scope. The collection site image and group image around the microscope should be pasted in the notes section of your slide.

- For the invertebrate collected, you must provide a photograph of the collection site and then provide an image of the specimen in the collection jar at the collection site. This second image must contain your group's IDs.

Timeline

The group presentation due date and format will be determined by the instructor.

NOTE: If any group member does not complete his or her individual component by the deadline, he or she may be fired from the group and must complete all individual AND group components of the project individually.

Rubrics

There may be situations in which some loafing occurs during the collaboration phase begins, and you must plan for this. Develop rubrics that outline expectations and grading guidelines for students. Rubrics that allow for individual grading of group members can be used to adjust for a lack of participation (Morgan, et al., 2014). You may have several rubrics, one for each portion of the project. You'll need one for the individual portion, one for discussion (if you have one), one for the final group product and/or presentation, and one for a peer and self-review. Each of these should have a deadline associated with it as well. Periodic deadlines help reduce procrastination, and to ensure progress on the project.

I use rubrics in my courses as they provide so many benefits to students and instructors. Rubrics provide students with a set of high expectations, which is the sixth Principle of Good Practice (Chickering and Gamson, 1987). Students can measure their performance against the rubric and use it as a self-assessment, or use it as a form of peer review. Each of these is a form of feedback you can use as part of the fourth Principle of Good Practice (Chickering and Gamson, 1987). Rubrics can help students become more self-directed and reflective in their learning, and can help instructors gauge the effectiveness of their instruction (Luft, 1998). On the next page, I have included a sample rubric for the individual portion of the virtual collection project.

For this project, there was no graded discussion forum, just one provided for group communication. I typically use the same (or slightly modified if necessary) rubric for all discussions, whether part of a project or not. To see more about discussions, please refer to Section 7.5. I have also included a sample rubric for the group product of the virtual collection project. This rubric focuses on content of the project, which for this project was usually a slide presentation, although students could choose another format.

Figure 7.4B – Rubric – INDIVIDUAL Portion Ecology Virtual Collection

SCORE	Percent of Grade	Category	Instructions
	20%	Pictures	All photographs must be clear and the organism must be clearly identifiable. As some specimens require multiple photographs for proper documentation, all photos must be presented for full credit. At least one photograph for each specimen must include your (and/or your group's) Blinn ID. Each photograph must also meet the requirements for species criteria (living at time of collection and native).
	10%	Taxon List and Category List	The specimens must accurately represent all items included under the taxon and category lists.
	5%	Domain	This should list the domain to which each organism belongs.
	5%	Kingdom	This should list the kingdom to which each organism belongs.

	5%	Phylum	This should list the phylum to which each organism belongs.
	5%	Class	This should list the class to which each organism belongs.
	5%	Other Taxonomic Designation	This should list any other taxonomic designations required by your professor (e.g. correct common name and/or scientific name).
	5%	Collection Information	All photographs must include the date, time, state, county, temperature, and weather conditions at time of collection. Additionally, you should provide a general description of the collection location.
	10%	Natural History Information	All photographs must include a description of the organism, its normal distribution, and its ecological role in its community.
	5%	References	References/citations for all natural history information as well as classification information must be included.

	20%	Presentation	The presentation must adequately include information on each specimen in the presentation and meet the length limits provided by your professor. The presentation must be coherent and well organized, and be consistent in format and style.
	5%	Organization & Neatness	This is college, and as such, you are expected to write at the college level. Please use proper grammar and spelling. The grammar/spelling tools on word processing software do not always catch mistakes. Do not use slang, text speak, contractions, etc. Format is up to you; just make sure that I can read your information and tell what the picture is.
TOTAL			

Figure Figure 7.4C - Rubric – GROUP Portion Ecology Virtual Collection

SCORE	Percent of Grade	Category	Instructions
	20%	Pictures	All photographs must be clear and the organism must be clearly identifiable. As some specimens require multiple photographs for proper documentation, all photos must be presented for full credit. At least one photograph for each specimen must include your (and/or your group's) Blinn ID. Each photograph must also meet the requirements for species criteria (living at time of collection and native).
	10%	Taxon List and Category List	The specimens must accurately represent all items included under the taxon and category lists.
	5%	Domain	This should list the domain to which each organism belongs.
	5%	Kingdom	This should list the kingdom to which each organism belongs.

	5%	Phylum	This should list the phylum to which each organism belongs.
	5%	Class	This should list the class to which each organism belongs.
	5%	Other Taxonomic Designation	This should list any other taxonomic designations required by your professor (e.g. correct common name and/or scientific name).
	5%	Collection Information	All photographs must include the date, time, state, county, temperature, and weather conditions at time of collection. Additionally, you should provide a general description of the collection location.
	10%	Natural History Information	All photographs must include a description of the organism, its normal distribution, and its ecological role in its community.
	5%	References	References/citations for all natural history information as well as classification information must be included.

	20%	Group Presenta-tion	The group presentation must adequately include information on each specimen in the presentation and meet the length limits provided by your professor. The presentation must be coherent and well organized, and consistent in style and format.
	5%	Organization & Neatness	This is college, and as such, you are expected to write at the college level. Please use proper grammar and spelling. The grammar/ spelling tools on word processing software do not always catch mistakes. Do not use slang, text speak, contractions, etc. Format is up to you; just make sure that I can read your information and tell what the picture is.

At my college, we measured soft skills such as communication and collaboration, so we added two more rubrics. The Presentation Rubric focused on the presentation of material, whether written or oral, while the Collaboration Rubric was used more as a peer and self-review. The final project consisted of an average of all the scores from each rubric. A sample Presentation Rubric and Collaboration Rubric are included here.

Figure 7.4D - Group Project Presentation Rubric

Category	0 Not Acceptable	1 Below Expectations	2 Appro
Organization	Presentation shows NO evidence of organization	Presentation shows little evidence of organization	Presenta dence o
Consistency	Presentation shows NO consistency between individual group members' contributions	Presentation shows little consistency between individual group members' contributions	Presenta tency be membe
Content	Presentation is significantly less than minimum length requirement	Presentation does NOT meet minimum length	Presenta length re is super
Accuracy	Presentation shows several instances of inaccuracy, and information is NOT thorough	Presentation shows several instances of inaccuracy, OR information is NOT thorough	Presenta stances informa
Spelling/ Pronunciation	Presentation shows several spelling or pronunciation errors	Presentation shows several spelling or pronunciation errors	Presenta ing or p
Sentence Structure & Language	Presentation shows several significant grammatical errors, and consistently uses language that is not professional	Presentation shows several significant grammatical errors, or consistently uses language that is not professional	Presenta cant gra language
Presentation Style	Presentation style is often awkward, vague, and/or choppy.	Presentation style is sometimes awkward, vague, and/or choppy.	Presenta function
Evaluation	**Category**	**Score**	**Group**
	Organization		1.
	Consistency		2.
	Content		3.
	Accuracy		4.
	Spelling/ Pronunciation		
	Sentence Structure & Language		
	Presentation Style		
Presentation Total			

ches Expectations	3 Meets Expectations	4 Exceeds Expectations
tion shows some evi- organization	Presentation shows obvious evidence of organization	Presentation shows obvious evidence of organization, and organization aids effectiveness of presentation
tion shows some consis- ween individual group ' contributions	Presentation shows obvious consistency between individual group members' contributions	Presentation shows obvious consistency between individual group members' contributions, and transitions are seamless
tion meets minimum quirements, but content cial	Presentation meets minimum length requirements, and content is substantive	Presentation exceeds minimum length requirement, and content is substantive and thoughtful
tion shows FEW in- f inaccuracy, OR some ion is NOT thorough	Presentation shows NO in-stances of inaccuracy	Presentation shows NO instances of inaccuracy, and information is thorough
tion shows several spell- onunciation errors	Presentation shows several spell-ing or pronunciation errors	Presentation shows several spell-ing or pronunciation errors
tion shows few signifi- nmatical errors, and uses that is professional	Presentation shows few sig-nificant grammatical errors, and consistently uses language that is professional	Presentation shows NO sig-nificant grammatical errors, and consistently uses language that is professional
tion style is clear and al.	Presentation style is always clear and functional, and is sometimes crisp, fluent, and precise.	Presentation style is always crisp, fluent, and precise.
Member Names:		

Figure 7.4E - Group Project Collaboration Rubric

Criteria	0 **Not Acceptable**	1 **Below Expectations**	2 App
Resources	Provided NO resources for information	Provided resources for information in works cited list but NO in-text citations	Prov tion i in-te
Communication	Provided NO feedback for other group members work	Provided feedback for few group members' work	Prov. grou
Contribution	Provided NO contributions to project presentation	Provided contributions in assembly, writing, and reviewing few parts of the presentation.	Prov assen most
Cooperation	Did NOT participate constructively in group meetings (Ex. Did not attend meetings, attended but never participated in discussions or work, consistently distracted group)	Participated constructively in few group meetings	Parti most
Leadership	Rejected all ideas from other group members Caused multiple problematic situations	Considered ideas from other group members, but did not suggest ideas Caused few problematic situation	Sugg other Caus
Evaluation		**Member 1**	Mer
	Resources		
	Communication		
	Contribution		
	Cooperation		
	Leadership		
Total			

oaches Expectations	3 **Meets Expectations**	4 **Exceeds Expectations**
ed resources for informa- works cited list AND citations	Provided resources for infor- mation in works cited list and in-text citations, and most are formatted correctly	Provided resources for infor- mation in works cited list and in-text citations, and all are reputable, reliable sources and are formatted correctly
ed feedback for most members' work	Provided timely, constructive feedback for all group members' work	Provided timely, constructive, and substantive feedback for all group members' work
ed timely contributions in ly, writing, and reviewing arts of the presentation.	Provided timely contributions in assembly, writing, and reviewing all parts of the presentation.	Provided timely, constructive, and substantive contribu- tions in assembly, writing, and reviewing all parts of the presentation.
ated constructively in roup meetings	Participated constructively in all group meetings	Participated constructively in all group meetings, took initia- tive to schedule meetings and encourage participation
ted ideas and considered roup members' ideas no problematic situations	Suggested ideas and considered other group members' ideas, Helped resolve problematic situations	Discussed ideas presented by other group members; asked questions for clarification, made suggestions for ways to use information in the final project Helped resolve problematic situations
ber 2	**Member 3**	**Member 4**

7.5 Discussion Forums

In your face-to-face courses, you probably ask students questions as you go through class, and discussions often naturally occur. In an online class, discussions need to be more carefully planned, but the benefits of discussions are worth the time required to plan them. Asynchronous online discussions are those in which students reply to a topic in a forum on the LMS during a specified window and then return to read and reply to peers' posts. This is different from face-to-face discussions in which students are all together and responding at the same time (synchronous).

Discussions are learning tools that build connections to students' prior experiences by asking students to talk about a topic and how it relates to their lives (Conaway and Zorn-Arnold, 2016). They support student understanding of course material by allowing students to share information gathered from outside resources, analyze opinions and research presented by others, and work in groups to construct their own knowledge. Online discussions are a way to encourage students to practice appropriate writing skills without instructors assigning papers or essays.

Provide examples of high- and lower-quality discussion posts (Sull, 2014). Discussions, if designed well, also allow students to be more self-directed in their learning by encouraging students to find an area of interest related to course material to research and use to support an opinion or idea (Baker, 2013). Students are exposed to multiple viewpoints, resources, and ideas, and are better able to analyze them. Students can benefit from the experiences of others by reading other students' discussion posts (Conaway and Zorn-Arnold, 2015). In this way, discussions support the Seventh Principle of Good Practice (Chickering and Gamson, 1987) by embracing student diversity. Andragogically, instructors function as designers of online discussions, and facilitators of learning by encouraging student to student and student to instructor interaction. This promotes social engagement as well as engagement with the course material. Instructors manage discussions by outlining and enforcing boundaries, encouraging participation, and assessing performance. To do all of this, instructors must become familiar with the LMS discussion tools to assist students with the technical aspects of online discussions.

Carefully plan asynchronous discussions for your online courses that include higher level questions without one set right or wrong answer.

We'll start with designing discussions that connect students to the course content. You'll need to pick a topic for each discussion. In a face-to-face class, you may ask questions that have one correct answer to see if students are paying attention or remember prior material. Don't do this in an online discussion. If students can Google the answers to questions, they will; so, in an online class you'll need to create better questions. Increase the level of complexity for your discussion questions (Refer to verbs associated with Revised Bloom's Taxonomy). In online discussions, you'll want to ask questions that are more open-ended, without one set right or wrong answer.

For example, I have used a discussion in which students are placed into groups of four. The group then chooses a case study to research from different viewpoints. One viewpoint asks students to take on the role of doctor and recommend a treatment. Another asks if the couple who carries a certain disease should have children or not. In other classes, I have asked questions on global warming. Students are always required to support their opinions with evidence, which also allows us to discuss sources of information that can be found on the Internet.

You can solicit informed opinions on topics, but make sure you have thoroughly explained content, grammar, and netiquette expectations. We want students to become better writers, so we must remind them of proper writing technique. Make sure you include your expectations in the instructions for every discussion forum. Also, give students feedback about their writing as part of your assessment. This feedback will not only increase student discussion skills, but also improve their writing skills.

 Teach students how to use the LMS discussion tool. Outline expectations and procedures in a discussion forum in which they get to know their classmates (and you).

Your first discussion forum can be an Icebreaker, and it's a fantastic way for everyone to get to know each other while introducing discussion expectations and procedures. It's a way for them to concentrate on learning how to use the learning management system (LMS) discussion tool, develop good discussion practices, and practice their writing with information they already know, rather than trying to do all of that and learn new material at the same time.

You'll be surprised at what students will share. I remember a student who said he had a tattoo of a baked potato. That sparked a discussion of tattoo ideas and favorite tattoo shops. Later, in another class, a student wrote, "I love killing animals! HaHa – I really just love to hunt. Don't hate me!" I remember reading that and thinking that kid has a dark sense of humor.

On the page opposite, you'll find instructions for an Icebreaker Discussion. On the following page, you'll find a sample discussion rubric for your reference.

Figure 7.5A – Sample Icebreaker Discussion Forum Instructions

Icebreaker Discussion

First post due by (Date & Time); All posts due by (Date & Time)

Directions:

The Icebreaker Discussion Assignment is designed to help you get to know your classmates. Your initial post is due by (Date & Time). You will not be able to see other students' posts until you have completed your first post (NOTE: this function is not available in all Learning Management Systems). We will have several discussion forums throughout the semester, so become familiar with the discussion rubric and instructions.

• Carefully read the instructions for each discussion forum.

• Complete required posts before each deadline.

• Completely answer all discussion questions, using examples, evidence, and research as needed.

• Respond thoughtfully and substantially, in a timely manner, to the minimum required number of peers' posts. (In a timely manner generally means within 48 hours.)

• Respond to questions and comments made to your posts in a timely manner.

• DO NOT post contact information in this forum. If you wish to contact me or fellow students, use the built-in email tool.

Icebreaker Discussion Questions:

Tell us about yourself, including the name you go by, your pronouns and where you are located.

• What is your major? What interests you about that?

• What are your future academic/career plans?

• What topics in biology interest you and why?

• Why are you taking this course online?

• What study tips do you have for other students?

To add your post, click on the "New Post" button above. Once you have completed your first post, you'll see other students posts display below. Click on each post to read and reply.

Figure 7.5B - Sample Discussion Rubric

Criteria	Exceeds Expectations	Meets Expectations	Approaches Expectations	Does Not Meet Expectations	Does Not Post
Student explains and supports opinions and ideas in discussion posts	Student thoroughly answered discussion question, and supported ideas and opinions using course materials and outside resources.	Student thoroughly answered discussion question, and supported ideas and opinions using course materials.	Student thoroughly answered discussion question.	Student attempted to answer discussion question, but does not fully explain ideas.	Student did not respond to discussion
Student engages in discussion and extends conversation with faculty and peers	Student exceeded the minimum number of substantive and timely responses to peers and faculty.	Student posted the minimum number of substantive and timely responses to peers and faculty.	Student posted the minimum number of timely responses to peers and faculty, but posts were not substantive, OR Student posted the minimum number of substantive responses to peers and faculty, but posts were not timely.	Student did not meet the minimum number of posts.	Student did not respond to peer and faculty posts.

You'll need to decide how many discussions you want to have during a semester. One each week may sound good, until you start reading all the student posts and realize how much time that requires. It also requires a lot of time on the part of your students. I suggest one about every three weeks or so, depending on the length of your class. Whatever you decide about number, make the discussions occur on a regular basis so that students know when to expect them. This gives students ample time to respond to each forum, and gives you about a week to grade each one.

Once you decide how many discussions you want to have in your course, and the topic of each, you'll need to decide how you plan to grade the discussions. Give a separate grade to each discussion, and then you can average them together to form a small part of the semester average. If discussion forms the majority of student activity in the course, the percentage of the course average should be higher.

Next, you'll need a rubric to grade the discussions. There are many discussion rubrics you can view on the Internet, and you can write your own rubric based on what you like about those. Remember to be very specific in your instructions and rubric so that there is less confusion.

- When do students need to have completed their initial post?

- How many replies to peers do students need to write?

- Can they do all their posts at one time, or must they be spread out over multiple days?

- Do students need to include links to information they discuss in their posts?

- What are your grammar expectations?

- What are your netiquette expectations?

- What are your content expectations?

You'll probably get a lot of questions about how long discussion posts need to be, at least at first. I usually don't put in a required length for posts, since some students are very concise, while others are not. I tell students I look for content and how students support their ideas rather than a specific number of sentences. I then must define the type of content I would like to see in a discussion post. I always respond to the Icebreaker discussion first so that students can use my post as a model for what and how they need to post. With a model post as feedback, students will get learn to better develop and support their ideas, as well as the technical aspects of their writing. You can also post examples of student posts from prior semesters, along with explanations about their quality (Sull, 2014).

 In online classes, making your presence felt in your course, especially in discussions, is teaching from the Power Zone. When teaching face-to-face courses, you need to spend most time in the Power Zone, which is the center of the action in the classroom. Instead of teaching from the desk or the front of the room, being in the center of the students facilitates classroom management and learning (Cain and Laird, 2011). However, online instructors must walk a fine line. Just like standing beside a student will influence their behavior and can begin to make them feel uncomfortable, dominating the discussion or offering negative feedback can make online students uncomfortable and less likely to share their thoughts (Sull, 2014). Your students won't likely post every day, and you don't have to do so either. Occasionally, you'll need to take a break and recharge as well (Sull, 2014).

CHAPTER 8
HOW TO CONSTRUCT AN EFFECTIVE ONLINE COURSE SYLLABUS

8.1 Similarities and Differences Between Face-to-Face and Online Syllabi

For more than two decades, the syllabus has been viewed as a contract between an instructor and his or her students. Matejka and Kurke even suggested adding a signature statement to the end of the syllabus for students to acknowledge they have read, understood, and will adhere to the guidelines in the syllabus. Syllabi can also be used to communicate your thoughts and head off student questions, as well as presenting a tone for the course (Matejka and Kurke, 1994).

 Check with your department head about a syllabus template for online courses. If your college offers a template for syllabi for online courses, it will likely contain all current college policies (specific to online courses or not), and that can save a lot of time.

Syllabi are standard for college courses, and there are standard components of syllabi that are common to all formats and subject of courses. A syllabus provides students with an overview of the entire course, from information about the instructor, to topics covered during the semester. A well-developed syllabus serves multiple purposes and assists the instructor in meeting motivational, structural, and evidentiary goals (Slattery and Carlson, 2005).

Faculty must prepare detailed syllabi to eliminate as much student confusion as possible and this ensures that all types of students can, as much as possible, equally access the course and have similar opportunity for success. Students benefit from knowing as much as possible about each course in which they are enrolled, so they can better manage their time and understand what they need to do to earn the grade they want (Slattery and Carlson, 2005).

Start with a syllabus from a face-to-face class if you don't have a template for an online course syllabus. As you teach more online courses, note questions you receive from students or issues that can be solved by modifying language in the syllabus. No syllabus will be perfect, but you can tweak items to make the syllabus clearer for students.

A face-to-face syllabus will give the location and times of the class. For an online class, you must be very explicit if there are any face-to-face requirements, and if so, where and when they will be. You must also define the consequences of absences from those face-to-face times. For example, in Texas, up to 15 percent of instructional time in "online" classes can be face-to-face, which would include orientation, labs, reviews, or tests (Distance Education Policies, Procedures, and Forms, 2017). Other states' rules may vary, so check to determine if any face-to-face components can be included in your online course.

Instructors often include expectations about behavior in their face-to-face course syllabi. You'll need different information in your online course syllabus. Students can't be tardy to online courses; it won't matter if they are talking or have their phone out while they are listening to a lecture or working on assignments, unless they are taking an exam.

For online classes, provide the syllabus information in two formats. Provide a PDF file in case students would like to print a copy of the syllabus. In addition, break up the syllabus into parts (based on section headers of the syllabus file) that are posted to the LMS. This allows online students to easily read and refer back to different sections online. You can link directly to college policies from the LMS as well, which means you won't have to update the information in the syllabus each time a policy changes. You'll only have to make sure the links still work.

A syllabus clarifies procedures, policies, assignments, grades, and other expectations for students and instructors. Each college may have a slightly different template for syllabi, but there are some items that should be included in every syllabus. These are discussed in the sections that follow, with modifications for online classes suggested as needed.

8.2 Course and Instructor Information

Course Information

A syllabus should clearly identify the course name, description, section number, semester and year. This is important for online courses, because students will read the syllabus individually rather than in a face-to-face class on the first day of the semester. Having the identifying information at the beginning of the syllabus reassures students that they have the correct, current syllabus for the course in which they are enrolled. Your syllabus course description should include the course description provided in the college catalog, as well as specific information about the online format of the course.

Include prerequisites for all courses. For example, for online courses colleges may require an online orientation to ensure that students have the technical skill required to be successful. List expected technical skills in this section as well, such as searching the Internet, downloading and uploading files, taking a screenshot and/or using software like Microsoft Word, PowerPoint, Adobe Reader, etc....

Instructor Information

All syllabi should include instructor contact information: email address, office phone number, office location and office hours. Most of my students contact me via email, and I have work emails forwarded to my smartphone. You will want to do this too, so you can address student questions as quickly as possible. My "official" response time to student emails (as stated in the syllabus) was the maximum time allowed by the college: 24 hours, except weekends and holidays. Your college might have a maximum response time, as well. I check emails once or twice a day and stay within my stated response time. You can always reply more quickly, but having a statement about response time in your syllabus allows you to unplug when necessary. Because you'll set up your course email on your phone, you'll want to make sure your students put "emergency" or "urgent" in the email subject line if they need an immediate response.

 As an online science instructor, if you drop everything for every email you receive from a student, your life will quickly become chaotic. Develop a triage system for emails, so you address urgent requests immediately. Other requests wait until a designated time to return emails that day.

Just as in a face-to-face course, you need to be available for your students. However, your online students likely won't be able to stop by your office on campus, even if you have one. Still, you must have "office hours," times that you are available for students in some way, and you must make students aware of these times in your syllabus and course shell. Outline how students can contact you and when, as well as a timeframe in which students can expect a response.

In your syllabus, include all the methods students can use to contact you, and when they are most likely to be able to reach you via each method. Your email address and average response time is essential. Other alternatives, such as Skype, Google Voice, and/ or Zoom are extremely helpful. For example, suppose you plan to be available from 10 a.m. until noon on Mondays and Thursdays. Set up an online meeting space such as Blackboard Collaborate or Zoom, and include in the syllabus information about how students can access the online meeting. Another option would be to state that students can email you for an appointment to meet online.

Instructors also give students their cell phone numbers, and let students know the instructor would answer texts and calls between certain hours on certain days of the week. In my experience, students don't abuse the privilege, and this contact option can help students resolve questions very quickly compared to email or setting an appointment for a Zoom or Skype session.

If you have reservations about giving your cell phone number to students, here's a solution: Google Voice. Sign up for Google Voice and you'll get a phone number that you can forward to your cell phone or other work number. You can make and receive calls and text messages through Google Voice, and you can select different phones to forward calls to based on the time of day or who the caller is. You can also set the Google Voice phone number to "Do Not Disturb." Phone calls to that number go straight to voicemail (Google Voice Features).

Required Course Materials

This section of the syllabus will include information about adopted textbook options, online learning systems, lab kit/simulation subscriptions, and any other required materials. For online students, it is helpful to tell students where they can go to purchase the materials since they may not be able to travel to the campus bookstore. Also, you should include any software requirements students in your course will need to be able to complete online assignments. For a face-to-face course, you might not need this information, but it is vital for online students, since students without the software, a computer, or high-speed Internet access might not be able to complete the course or not do as well in the course (West and Shoemaker, 2012).

For example, if students in your course will be completing a writing assignment, will they need to complete it in Microsoft Word, or can they use another word processing software? Do they need to convert all of their files to PDF before uploading? Compatibility issues can arise when everyone is using different software. Include a browser recommendation for use with the learning management system, and a reminder that not everything on the Internet is compatible with every browser. I often have students submit picture evidence of their experiments, so I include a digital camera as a requirement, but emphasize that a camera on a smartphone will work.

Learning Objectives

These will not differ between your face-to-face course and your online course. Include your learning objectives from the "lecture" portion and lab portion of your course. It is important to include the course objectives in the syllabus because it tells the students what they should learn in the course.

Course Calendar

This will be discussed in Chapter 9. As with any syllabus, include a statement that the calendar may be changed as needed during the semester.

8.3 Course Grading Information

Instructional Methods

In all syllabi, it is a best practice to include the rationale behind the assignments and instructional activities in your course.

Assignment Descriptions

Different requirements could exist for this section of the syllabus, but it probably will not differ much, if any, from your face-to-face syllabus. You should at least include a description of each category of assignment, like quizzes or discussions, and the weight of each category and major assignment.

Grading Criteria & Grade Scale

Students in online classes will have the same questions about grading as students in face-to-face classes, and possibly more. All students will want to know what the grade scale is, and what grade is required to earn an A, B, C, etc. Students in online classes want to know what parts of the course are graded and which are not, and what percentage of the course average each assignment will be. They will also have questions about how assignments will be submitted and graded. For example, if students write a paper, they can upload it to a dropbox in the LMS. Will you also accept it if they email you the paper? I suggest you include a statement in your syllabus that all assignments must be submitted through the LMS so that you have a record of the assignment. Also, you won't have to look in multiple places for student assignment submissions. For those rare instances in which an LMS outage coincides with a deadline, you might also include an emergency procedure.

Since many assignments in online courses can be computer graded, it is important to also include a statement in your syllabus about the time required to grade different types of assignments. For example, you may state that computer graded quizzes will display a grade immediately, unless there is a question that must be graded by the instructor. For quizzes, I recommend writing questions that can be computer graded, and include feedback as discussed in Chapter 13. This will save you time, since any lab report or other instructor graded assignment will take more of your time.

A reminder of deadlines in the Grading section of your syllabus can be useful. Let students know what to expect if they miss deadlines, and arrange due dates for instructor graded assignments when you'll have enough time to grade them in in the time you specified in your syllabus. Always over-estimate the time it will take you to grade an assignment or test in case an emergency arises.

Academic Dishonesty

This section may not look very different from your face-to-face syllabus. Your college probably has a statement about academic integrity that is required in all syllabi. Students need to understand what constitutes academic dishonesty in an online course, and what safeguards are in place in your course to prevent academic dishonesty. We'll discuss academic dishonesty more in Chapter 14.

Exam Proctoring

You will want to require exam proctoring in some way. Consider the options described in Chapter 14, and explain the options you will allow students to use in your course. An example from one of my prior syllabi is below.

Figure 8.3A – Proctoring Exams

All exams must be taken in a proctored environment. The four approved proctoring mechanisms for exams in this course include:

1. At our College Testing Center.

2. At another college or university testing center (must be pre-approved by the instructor.).

3. Via an online proctoring service.

4. Respondus Monitor test proctoring software

Details regarding the deadlines and procedures involved with each proctoring option will be provided in the Learning Management System. Students must inform instructor of their proctoring choice no later than two weeks prior to the opening of the first exam window so that test information can be sent to the appropriate proctor.

Late Work/Make-up Work

Regardless of course format, instructors must develop policies for how to deal with late work and make-up work. In an online course, your policies need to be very detailed, specific, and consistent. You'll have to define what constitutes late work in your online course, and in what situations students are allowed to make-up assignments and/or exams.

Michael Dalman, professor of geology at Blinn College, injects humor into his syllabus at this point. Here's a statement from one of his syllabi:

> No late Exams, lab reports, Mastering Geology assignments or online discussions will be accepted. If you are anticipating computer glitches, being the victim of street crime, bad planning, a Senate filibuster, embarrassing messages from "MOM" on your Instagram or Discord, animal attacks, hurtful comments by your close friends, good lovin' gone bad, terrorism, a disappointing credit report, seeing your new brother in law on Live PD, an unanticipated appearance on Maury Povich, being struck by space junk, unforeseen cataclysmic acts of God, suburban malaise, urban ennui, funding cuts for higher education, a date ending with a interview by Chris Hansen, the paralysis of analysis, rude tweets, infected Terrible Towel burns, trouble with your Tesla charging station, loss of hope in your audacity or vice versa, the debilitating shame of buying a Justin Bieber song, undergoing enhanced interrogation techniques, dating a Kardashian, losing your science mojo, or anything else that might interfere with your Exams, Lab Reports, and online work, Get your work started early, and turn them in early! (Dalman, 2017)

8.4 Attendance

The Ohio Department of Education recently performed attendance audits on online schools. Ohio's largest online school, the Electronic Classroom of Tomorrow (ECOT), is currently in a legal battle with the state because the attendance audit found online students were logging into the school's online system about one hour per day. If the state uses log-in time as documentation of attendance, ECOT could potentially lose $80 million dollars in funding. And ECOT is not alone. Several other online schools in Ohio could lose funding as well (Siegel, 2016).

ECOT and other charter schools are challenging the audits for several reasons. Several schools' learning management software platforms do not report total time spent in courses. Of those systems that do report total log in times, those totals do not always match the time spent actively engaged in activities. Also, time spent on non-computer activities was not recorded in learning logs (Siegel, 2016). The battle continues between these online schools and the Ohio Department of Education, and a simple resolution seems unlikely. With attendance tied to funding, however, online schools need to develop a process of recording accurate attendance that will satisfy state education agencies.

While the previous example dealt with K-12 schools, could this situation ever arise for colleges regarding their online courses? Perhaps. In Texas, a large portion of community college funding is tied to the total number of contact hours, which represent scheduled instructional time (Legislative Budget Board Staff, 2016). For face-to-face classes, class schedules in syllabi make it fairly simple to account for the number of contact hours per course. For example, if a class meets for 3 hours per week for 16 weeks, that totals 48 contact hours. However, how do we calculate contact hours for online college courses? Logic suggests that if an online course is equivalent in rigor, activities, and assessment to a face-to-face class, then the online course would have an equivalent number of contact hours. However, what if colleges are audited for contact hours the way public schools are audited for attendance? Could contact hours of online courses be questioned?

 Your college may have a standard attendance policy. However, that attendance policy may be open to interpretation for online courses. Develop a detailed attendance policy for your online course.

Even if your college does not have a minimum attendance policy, you should outline your expectations for attendance/participation in your online course and consequences if students do not meet these expectations.

Why should you have an attendance policy? Not requiring attendance in face-to-face classes tends to increase absences, and increased absences has a negative effect on student success (Levine, 1992). In undergraduate biology courses, students at the beginning of a semester predict high grades along with high attendance. However, average attendance at the end of the semester averaged 70% (Moore, 2003). If the same trend applies to online science courses, it is likely that your students will plan to spend a lot of time engaged in the course, but that plan may not come to fruition.

Several reports demonstrate a correlation between attendance and grades in science courses. In face-to-face undergraduate biology courses, 95 percent of students who attended 81-100 percent of classes earned a grade of C or better in their course. However, attendance at the end of the semester averaged 70 percent (Moore, 2003). Freeman, et al. (2007) also showed a correlation between attendance and success in biology classes.

A study of chemistry students at two universities (Southern Arkansas University and Cochise College) also demonstrated that attendance is related to success. Over 70 percent of students who attended 95 percent or more of classes earned a grade of B or above at both colleges, which suggests encouraging attendance can help students achieve success (Lyubartseva and Mallik, 2012). In face-to-face cell biology classes, 44 percent of students who scored a grade of C or better missed no classes, and 27 percent attended at least 90 percent of classes. Attendance had more influence on passing the course than having a high GPA (Soto and Sulekha, 2009).

Some instructors choose submission of assignments as a measure of participation and attendance. Using a 25 percent threshold of absences, a student could be administratively withdrawn from an online course if they fail to submit 25 percent of graded assignments. To report absences, an instructor would simply need to keep track of the number of zeros in the gradebook for each student.

Another method of tracking participation and attendance is the number of log-ins per week. For example, instructors could require students to log into the learning management system three times per week. Learning management systems typically track the number of log-ins, and even record days and times. An instructor could pull a report each week to determine if students are meeting the minimum log-in requirement. However, simply logging into the LMS does not mean that the student is completing work. This is somewhat similar to students who attend face-to-face classes but sleep through class.

Most learning management systems track the time a student spends logged into the system. But again, logging in does not necessarily mean a student is engaged in the class material. Also, depending on how instructors build their course in the LMS, some items may open in browser windows outside of the LMS, and time spent on that material may not be recorded. It also does not account for work done outside the LMS, like doing research, experiments, or writing papers.

Whatever method of tracking attendance and participation you choose, make sure you describe the method of taking attendance and how attendance is related to success. Emphasizing time on task is the Fifth Principle of Good Practice (Chickering and Gamson, 1987), and in an online course, time on task is directly related to attendance. Instructors should contact students immediately when they miss deadlines or begin to show a lack of participation. A study of college freshmen in English classes demonstrated that instructor contact significantly increased grades and decreased absences (Richie and Hargrove, 2004).

8.5 Student and Faculty Time Management Tips

Online students face a lot of distractions, much like online instructors. Some days, it will seem like you simply cannot get anything done because of interruptions. Your students may have less experience with time management and online classes than you, so you can share your experiences with them. A few characteristics are common between good students in all types and formats of classes. It may sound obvious, but students in online classes need reminders and advice that you would normally give to your face-to-face classes.

As instructors, we teach so much more than just our subject material. Students often do not know how to study or manage their time. It is our job to help students learn these skills as well. Students in online classes need to know what they are getting themselves into. They need to know everything they will have to do for the course at the beginning of the semester. That way they can adjust their schedules so they won't get behind. Recommend that students put all of the course deadlines and due dates and times in their calendars – whatever type of calendar they use. I like to tell students to put in reminders in their phones before the deadlines and due dates so they have time to do something about it if they have not completed everything.

Just like any other class, students should designate study times throughout the week and keep to a schedule. Keep in mind that, just like us, their schedules might change from week to week. Students need to plan week to week to ensure that they not only get everything done, but they also study little bits at a time. We all know cramming for exams doesn't typically work, especially for science classes. Remind your students of this. It will be tempting for online students to procrastinate and/or try to do everything for a unit right before the unit deadline. Tell students to break up the work, and check into the class daily if possible.

Remind students of upcoming assignments, tests, and projects. For example, I have several long-term assignments in each of my classes. I have reminders built into my calendar so that students will remember to work on those projects a little at a time. I also have progress checks throughout the semester to ensure students are on track. I have them submit sources with summaries or a rough draft. Students will do better because they don't wait until the last minute to complete the assignment, and because they receive feedback on the progress checks.

The quality of your planning and course development will impact how much time you will need to spend on course facilitation during the semester. Planning is the first step in time management. Clear instructions, consistent organization, and easy course navigation will reduce the amount of time you'll spend answering the same student questions.

Speaking of student questions, each time you facilitate a course, make note of questions students ask. You can tweak assignment instructions for future classes based on student questions, and/or compile questions into a Frequently Asked Questions list for your classes. You can point students to the FAQs rather than answering redundant questions.

Students in online classes can access their online courses 24 hours per day, 7 days a week. Because of this, students can sometimes expect to be able to contact their instructors 24 hours per day, 7 days a week. This is only partially true, and students need to be reminded of this. Remind students that they can email you anytime they wish, but you'll also need to tell them when they can expect a response from you.

Just like online students, online instructors need to set aside time each day for their classes. You would normally meet with each class for six hours of class time in a face-to-face class, so plan on spending that much time each week facilitating your online classes. Walk students through the process you use to create your weekly schedule, so they can use that as a model to create their own weekly schedule and estimate the amount of time they'll need to devote to class each week.

Tell students, in general terms, when you are available for online appointments. For example, you may simply state that appointments may be scheduled by email within the hours of 9 a.m. and 7 p.m.,

Monday through Saturday. Alternatively, you may make standing online appointments that students can join online. This makes it convenient for students, but you may be sitting by the computer (like sitting in your office), and have no students contact you during that time. If students don't stop by your online "office hours", you can get other work done, like emailing reminders or grading.

Instructors can easily become overwhelmed, spending so much time teaching, grading, and worrying about their students that their own lives take a back seat. We want to avoid this by careful planning and organization. Set aside specific times each week to answer emails, post to discussions, grade assignments, and otherwise interact with your students. Send updates at least weekly to students, reminding them of what is to be done that week and what is upcoming. I send a weekly email and include the calendar for the next week. It doesn't take long to copy the calendar for the upcoming week and remind students to keep working on longer term projects.

8.6 Technology Back-up Plan

Technology will fail; it's just a question of when. Sometimes, it seems like it fails at the worst possible time. Knowing this, we and our students need to have contingency plans. This summer, my Internet was down for two days, so I had to find another Internet source. I spent 4 hours each day at Starbucks, drinking free refills of iced coffee and tea. There are solutions; students just don't always think about them. They can go to campus and use the computers and Internet in computer labs or the library. If it's just an Internet problem, students can go to a friend's house, a local library, campus, or a café.

In your syllabus, you should include a statement informing students that due dates and deadlines will not be adjusted due to technical difficulties. You can add it into the Late Work section of your syllabus and address other potential causes of late work at the same time.

 Always include information about potential LMS problems. At Blinn College and McLennan Community Col-

lege, I have received emails and announcements about downtimes for LMS maintenance. If you don't know how your college communicates this information to faculty and students, ask the technology or distance learning department. Then, pass this information along to your students. You might get a student who says the LMS was not working for them, and this will let you know if the issue was with the LMS or on the student's end.

8.7 Student Resources & Support

LMS Support

Include contact information and links to tutorials for students when they have questions or problems with the learning management system. I have included links to LMS support pages in Chapter 10, since you'll want to include those on your course page. However, include them in the syllabus too, in case students can't log into the LMS.

Technical Assistance

Most colleges have a technology department that can help students with software or hardware questions. Include this information in your syllabus and on your course page.

Library Access

Online students will still need to access library services, so include a link to the library page. Also include brief instructions on how to log into the library search engine.

Disability Services & ADA Statement

All syllabi need a statement about the Americans with Disabilities Act. Your college is required to provide information about disability services to students, so include that information in your syllabus. You can link directly to your college's Office of Disabilities Services Page from your syllabus and your course page.

CHAPTER 9
ORGANIZATION IS KEY

9.1 Course Organization
Linear vs. Modular

The organization of your online course dictates the success of your course, so consider carefully. I will discuss two options for organization within the Learning Management System (LMS): Linear and Modular. I have seen both used successfully and can tell you that the organization plan instructors choose reflects the variety of the content in their courses.

A modular organization style breaks up course content into types of content. For example, quizzes would all be together in a quiz folder. Videos would be in a separate folder, assignments in another folder, and the textbook resources in the textbook online learning system. When the calendar tells students to read a certain chapter and complete tutorials, it would also need to indicate to students where to find the materials. Think about all the times a student has asked you where something was in the classroom, even after you already told the class. Can you imagine what it would be like online when students can't find something? Many will ask, but some will simply email you right before or after the deadline that they couldn't find something.

A linear organization style aligns content by date, and this style is more common. I prefer this organization plan, since it seems easier to me for students to click on the first unit and have everything they need to complete in one folder whenever possible. Here's the problem: it is not always possible to have everything students need to complete together in place. For example, students will still need to read the textbook chapters, access the textbook online learning system, and perform lab activities. When building your course in the Learning Management System, you'll still need to refer and/or link to these items inside your linear content folders.

To ensure students know what they are supposed to do and when they are supposed to do it, you need a detailed and specific calendar. How detailed will depend on whether you employ a modular or linear organization style. A calendar for a course based on modular organization will need to include information about where to find everything for that week on the calendar, in addition to what students are supposed to do and the weekly deadlines. In the next section, we'll discuss how to transition from a simple face-to-face calendar to a detailed calendar for your online class.

Each LMS is customizable, so what you see in your course shell will be different from the icons I have in my examples. The information and consistency is most important, so that students know what to do and how to do it. Focus on how to organize your content (what you put in your course calendar) into manageable chunks that students can digest each week.

In a linear organization plan, you'll organize by Unit and Week. On my sample linear calendar on the next page, Unit 1 consists of 4 weeks of material and the Unit 1 Exam. I have included a sample Unit 1 folder here.

Linear

Figure 9.1A – Sample Linear LMS Organization Unit Folder

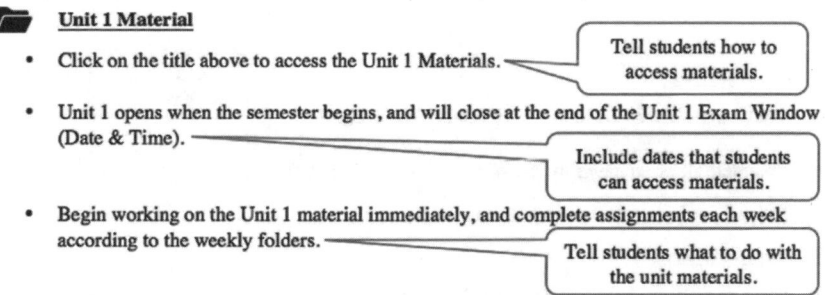

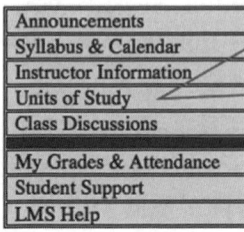

In a linear organization plan, all the course content is contained under one main section of the LMS. Depending on the type of LMS, the buttons may be across the top instead of on the left side of the screen. The labels can be changed as well.

Figure 9.1B – Sample Main Selection Button

 The icons will differ depending on your LMS and how much you can customize your course shell, but you should always tell students what to do and how to do it. You'll see in the sample Unit 1 Folder Information (Figure (9.1A), that I have included how to access the materials, what to do once students access the materials, and the deadlines.

Figure 9.1C – Linear LMS Organization Weekly Learning Modules (Inside Unit 1 Folder)

📁Week 1 Material

- Click on the title above to access the Unit 1 Materials. ⟶ Tell students how to access materials.

- Complete all assignments by the Week 1 deadline (Date & Time).

📁Week 2 Material

- Click on the title above to access the Unit 1 Materials. ⟶ Tell students the deadline for each week.

- Complete all assignments by the Week 1 deadline (Date & Time).

📁Week 3 Material

Keep the format consistent from week to week.

- Click on the title above to access the Unit 1 Materials.

- Complete all assignments by the Week 1 deadline (Date & Time).

📁Week 4 Material

- Click on the title above to access the Unit 1 Materials.

- Complete all assignments by the Week 1 deadline (Date & Time). ⟶ Include exam window information so students can plan ahead.

- NOTE: Unit 1 Exam Window: (Dates & Times of Opening and Closing.)

Include some information and reminders along with the folder, explaining what students should do. Once students follow instructions and click on the Unit 1 Folder, they are taken to the weekly folders within that unit, which contain notes, videos, quizzes, discussions, etc... You don't have to group the weekly material within unit folders, but I group it together that way so that there are fewer questions about what material is covered on each exam. It's simple to tell students that the material in Unit 1 is covered on the Unit 1 Exam.

Modular

If you choose a modular organization plan, your LMS organization will look very different, but you should still include what the students should do and how they should do it. Since a modular design groups like items, you won't have materials within Unit or Week folders. Instead, you'll have Week or Unit folders inside Materials folders. Students would use your course calendar to know what to do each week, and know where to go to access the material based on the corresponding section labels.

Some instructors choose to open all quizzes, dropboxes, and exams on the first day of the course, and have each close at certain points in the semester. Others will open and close items each week during the semester. You'll need to decide which works best for your course and your students. I typically open all quizzes and dropboxes at the beginning of the semester, but have more specific exam windows in which the exam can be taken. I do this to allow students the flexibility to work ahead if needed, but also to help ensure test security and allow me an opportunity to discuss the exam with students at more scheduled times.

Once you have decided which organization pattern to use, create all the folders and sub-folders you'll need based on your course calendar of assignments. I suggest creating one major unit folder and instruction information, and then creating weekly folders within it. Choose a font that is large enough to be easily read, and keep your format and information consistent between each folder. To help with consistency, you can then copy each folder. Again, how to do this will vary depending on the LMS, so search the Help section in your LMS for how to copy a folder or learning module. Once you have enough weekly folders in your Unit folder, you can then copy the unit folder and it will copy the weekly folders within it at the same time. Then, all you must do is edit the folder information. All your folders will have the same pattern of organization and information, and the text in your LMS course won't look like it came from a ransom note.

Figure 9.1D – Modular Organization Plan in LMS and Course Calendar

Week	What to do this week & Where to find it:
Week 1 – Aug. XX – Aug. XX	**Learning Objectives:** • To identify correct laboratory safety procedures. • To identify parts of a graph. • To interpret data contained in bar graphs. • To use the scientific method to search for explanations of nature. **Textbook Reading Assignment:** • Chapter 1, Section 1 – (include link to textbook or how to access it from LMS) **Videos & Animations:** • Lab Safety Video **Discussion:** • Icebreaker Discussion **Assignments:** • Zombie College Lab Safety Activity • Safety Contract Submission (**Materials below will appear only after the Safety Contract has been submitted.**) • Interpreting Bar Graphs Exercise • Scientific Method Lab Report **ONLINE ASSIGNMENT DEADLINE – Monday, August XX at (specify time)**

Each of these headings corresponds to a major content area of the modular LMS course shell.

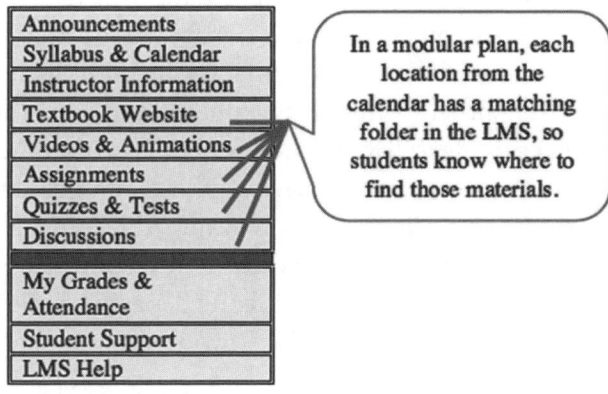

Announcements
Syllabus & Calendar
Instructor Information
Textbook Website
Videos & Animations
Assignments
Quizzes & Tests
Discussions

My Grades & Attendance
Student Support
LMS Help

In a modular plan, each location from the calendar has a matching folder in the LMS, so students know where to find those materials.

9.2 Building a Better Calendar

Prepare a detailed calendar for your course so you and your students know what to do, when to do it, and how to access all materials.

A linear online calendar is divided by unit and week, which would correspond to the content folders of the LMS. It includes learning objectives, graded assignments, and the deadline. In my sample calendars, notice that I have weeks identified by date, so there is no confusion about what is to be completed when. Students can complete the work over any number of days during that week, but having everything listed on the calendar allows students to see how much work there is to do each week, and where to find it. I organize my course in the LMS the same way I organize the course in the calendar so there is less confusion for the students.

A calendar based on a modular organization plan has many of the same characteristics of the linear calendar, such as learning objectives, graded assignments, and deadlines. However, it also must contain any non-graded tasks students should complete, such as reading the textbook or watching videos. You'll have to separate tasks according to where the student must go to complete the task, since distinct types of items will be in separate places, including outside of the LMS. I have included the same week of material in the modular calendar in Figure 9.2A but have only highlighted the differences from the linear calendar. I have found that different colleges may require different information in the syllabus course calendar. At McLennan Community College, many instructors do not include dates on the syllabus course calendar so that they do not have to keep updating it every semester. They just update the dates in the LMS. At Blinn College, we were required to put dates in our calendar on the syllabus, as well as how many contact hours each date represented. Make sure you ask your department head about requirements for the course calendar in your syllabus.

 Adult learners appreciate the control and flexibility they have in online classes because it feeds into their self-directedness (Conaway and Zorn-Arnold, 2015). However, instructors must give students tools to help them manage their time and plan when to work on course material each week. A detailed calendar containing all instructional tasks, assignments and deadlines is one of those tools.

Because I have taught my science courses for so long, I'm practiced at creating a semester schedule and not falling behind. When I first started teaching, it was difficult to know just how much time each activity would take. When I implement a new activity, I always allot more time than I think I might need. Once the class has completed the activity, I record the actual time required for later reference.

For your online class, keep careful track of time so that you're not assigning too many hours of work each week. Watching your lectures, participating in discussions, completing quizzes, watching videos, and completing laboratory activities all count toward the time students would be in "class." Remember that the typical contact hours for a four-credit science course include three hours of "lecture" (class time) and three hours of lab time each week. Analyze the time required in your course to give students an accurate estimation of time they will need to spend completing the work in your class each week. This practice supports the Fifth Principle of Good Practice: time on task (Chickering and

Figure 9.2A – Sample Modular Calendar

Week	What to do this week & Where to find it:

Week 1 –
 	
Aug XX –
X
	Learning Objectives:
	• To identify correct laboratory safety procedures.
	• To identify parts of a graph.
	• To interpret data contained in bar graphs.
	• To use the scientific method to search for explanations of nature.
	
	Textbook Reading Assignment:
	  • Chapter 1, Section 1 – (include link to textbook or how to access it from LMS)
	
	Videos & Animations:
	  • Lab Safety Video
	
	Discussion:
	  • Icebreaker Discussion
	
	Assignments:
	• Zombie College Lab Safety Activity
	• Safety Contract Submission (**Materials below will appear only after the Safety Contract has been submitted.**)
	• Interpreting Bar Graphs Exercise
	• Scientific Method Lab Report
	
	ONLINE ASSIGNMENT DEADLINE – Monday, August XX at (specify time)

Each of these headings corresponds to a major content area of the modular LMS course shell.

Gamson, 1987).

On the next page, I have included a sample basic calendar for a face-to-face biology course so you can view the transformation from a simple face-to-face calendar to a detailed calendar for online classes.

Figure 9.2B – Sample Face-to-Face Calendar

Date	Lecture Topic	Lab Topic
Aug. 29	Introduction, Pre-test	Lab Safety
Aug. 31	Ch 1: Introduction	Scientific Method
Sept. 2	The Metric System	
Sept. 5	The Metric System	Metric System
Sept. 7	Ch 2: Chemical Context of Life	
Sept. 9	Ch 3: Water	Water
Sept. 12	Ch 3: Continued	Water
Sept. 14	Ch 4: Carbon Ch 5: Organic Molecules	
Sept. 16	Ch 5: Continued	Organic Molecules
Sept. 19	Ch 5: Continued	Organic Molecules
Sept. 21	**Lecture Exam 1**	
Sept. 23	**Lab Exam 1**	

The calendar in Figure 9.2B is basic, and arranged by class day. It includes major due dates and general topics only, because in class you will give specific information. My online class calendar has more deadlines and detail, including all student tasks, whether graded or not.

In the calendar for your online course, include weekly deadlines to keep students on track. Having no weekly deadlines is a recipe for procrastination disaster. I have seen students in other courses wait until right before the end of the semester to complete everything because the end of the semester was the only deadline. (Can you imagine having to grade everything right before the end of the semester?) Pick a day and time for the graded assignments to close each week, and choose a time that you will be available to answer questions and handle "emergencies". Students will procrastinate, even on a weekly basis.

When I first started teaching online, I set an end of the week deadline of 11:59 p.m. on Sunday. Big mistake. I underestimated the procrastination potential of my students. I awoke Monday morning to multiple emails that had been sent late Sunday evening about the Internet problems with the quiz.

In subsequent semesters, I changed the deadline to a day and time during the week in which I was available for the prior hour. I then resolved issues students reported. Students still had flexibility in completing assignments during the week and problem reports decreased drastically. Whichever weekly deadline you choose, keep it the same throughout the semester so that there is no question about when access to quizzes and dropboxes will end.

As I began using a very detailed calendar, I found it benefitted all my courses, including face-to-face. It helped me plan lessons for each day of the course, kept me from getting behind as I went through the semester and ensured I met all student learning goals. My students knew what they should have been doing each week in the online course, and what we would do each class day in my face-to-face course. Having a detailed calendar also serves as a checklist for students. My course framework built in the LMS was created around my calendar, and we'll cover how to use your linear calendar to build your course in the LMS.

9.3 Exam Windows

Give students a window of time for each exam during the semester so they have ample opportunity to schedule each exam around their work and family schedule.

In a face-to-face class, students have a set time and date for each exam. In an online class, you'll need to have a window of time in which the exams are open. It needs to be long enough so that every student can find a time within the window to take the exam. I generally give students a window of several days in which to complete the test, including week days and weekend days. For my online classes, I combine lecture and lab material into one test. This can create a longer exam, but students would only have four exams total. This means they'll have to take fewer exams, and that can save them time and money on proctoring fees. And trust me, you want to have proctored exams in your online course.

Figure 9.3A – Sample Linear Exam Window Calendar

Unit 1 –	Week 4 –	Unit 1, Week 4
Weeks 1-4	Sept. XX – Sept. XX	**Learning Objectives:** • **Apply** scientific reasoning to investigate questions, and **analyze** data. • **Use** critical thinking and scientific problem solving. • **Summarize** effectively the results of scientific investigations.
Aug. XX – Sept. XX		
		Now it is time for you to STUDY for your first exam. The exam will cover everything in Weeks 1, 2, 3, and 4, including lecture and lab assignments. Schedule an appointment for your exam to be proctored during the exam window (if necessary).
		Graded Assignments for this unit: • Practice Test • Unit 1 Exam - Must be proctored
		Exam Window: 8am, Thursday, September 21, through 8pm, Monday, September 25
		ONLINE ASSIGNMENT DEADLINE – Monday, August XX at (specify time)

A reminder about what the exam will cover will decrease student questions.

Be specific about the exam window, including dates and times.

Decide how your exams will be proctored, and remind students to set appointment if necessary. See Chapter 14 for proctoring

Figure 9.3B – Sample Modular Exam Window Calendar

Unit 1 –	Week 4 –	Unit 1, Week 4
Weeks 1-4 Aug. XX – Sept. XX	Sept. XX – Sept. XX	**Learning Objectives:** • **Apply** scientific reasoning to investigate questions, and **analyze** data. • **Use** critical thinking and scientific problem solving. • **Summarize** effectively the results of scientific investigations. Now it is time for you to STUDY for your first exam. The exam will cover everything in Units 1, 2, 3, and 4, including lecture and lab assignments. Schedule an appointment for your exam to be proctored during the exam window (if necessary). **Assignments:** • Practice Test • Unit 1 Exam - Must be proctored Exam Window: 8am, Thursday, September 21, through 8pm, Monday, September 25 **ONLINE ASSIGNMENT DEADLINE** – Monday, **August XX at (specify time)**

> Practice test and Exam would be found under Quizzes/Tests in a modular organization plan.

SECTION III: FACILITATING THE COURSE

CHAPTER 10
ORIENTING STUDENTS TO THE COURSE

10.1 Welcome to Online Learning

Orienting students to your course can begin before the course. Some students may have questions or wonder what to expect from your course. Some may email you and ask for a syllabus, but more will likely suffer in silence. Based on questions I received about my online course, I developed an email to send students before each semester begins.

A welcome email helps head off questions from students and helps make certain students know what they are getting themselves into. You will want to use a similar strategy to help your students understand the practical differences between online and face-to-face courses. I have included a sample Welcome to Online Biology email here.

Figure 10.1A – Sample Welcome to Online Bio. Email

Welcome to Online Biology! This section is a fully online class, which means that you won't have to physically attend class. Sounds great! BUT, there are some things you need to understand about this course to do well, and you should consider these things when considering a fully online science course.

1. 100 percent of your time in this class will be spent off campus. You must be SELF-MOTIVATED and organized to stay on track, and complete assignments, labs, and exams on time to do well in this class.

2. Attendance will be taken in the online course. (Insert attendance policy here.)

3. Not everything you do in this course will be graded, but the non-graded content prepares you for and helps you do well on the graded content. The course schedule lists everything you'll need to complete each week, so you can use it as a checklist as you are completing course assignments. I suggest using the calendar function in your cell phone to set reminders of due dates and exam windows.

4. You WILL complete laboratory activities as part of this course. Each activity will have accompanying assignments, to ensure completion of the activity and check for understanding. You will be required to purchase (a lab kit, virtual lab subscription, lab materials, etc.) as part of the materials for this course, and that information will be contained in the syllabus distributed on the first day of class.

5. I do NOT recommend taking an online class if you do not have a reliable computer and Internet access. Also, if you live in a dormitory, you should check with your dorm administrator to make sure that you have a space in which you can complete the lab activities. Some chemicals used in labs may not be allowed in dorm rooms.

6. If your Internet goes down, you need to have a backup plan (friend's house, library, Internet café, etc.), as assignment due dates WILL NOT be adjusted due to technological issues.

7. You need to really know yourself and be honest with yourself about this class. Do you want to learn biology on a flexible schedule that allows you to work around family and work duties? Do you understand that a significant time investment will still be required? Are you here because you don't like sitting in class and want to get out of class as much as possible? Are you likely to forget assignments or procrastinate? Think about why you chose this online class, and how likely you are to complete the work required outside the classroom on schedule.

8. If some of you decide the online class is not for you, I understand and wish you the best. Just make sure you drop this course and add a different section within the time allotted by the college. For those of you who have weighed the options and have decided to continue with this class, I am here to help you all I can. Let's have a great semester!

10.2 Types of Orientations

Just as colleges have orientations to let students know where resources are and how to be successful, you'll need to orient your students to your LMS course shell, your course content and laboratory safety. Some students may rely on orientations more than others. Instructors must include information for students who have never taken an online class before, understanding that others who do not need such extensive assistance can ignore the orientation information they don't need. There are two basic types of orientations: video and written tutorials with screenshots. They each have advantages and disadvantages, and I recommend using each in various places in your LMS course.

Videos can demonstrate how to access materials or use equipment. They are fairly simple to make with a digital video camera or any of the screencasting software that I have mentioned earlier in this book. However, to make sure they are ADA accessible, you'll need to close-caption all of them. You can do this by uploading the videos to YouTube and using their closed-caption tool, but it takes time. It took me about 20 minutes to caption a 7 minute video I created. How long it takes for your videos will depend on how much and how fast you speak during your videos. Also, videos require more bandwidth than written tutorials with screenshots, which could increase Internet usage for you and your students.

Written tutorials with screenshots work well for simpler tasks students need to perform in the LMS, like downloading or uploading files. The first time students will complete a task, make sure that you explain to them how to complete that task. For example, you might need to show students how to attach an assignment to upload it to a dropbox, or you might need to show them how to reply to a discussion post. Pictures make it easier to explain these things. I use my computer's snipping tool to capture the images from the computer screen, but there are other options available, like Jing or Snagit.

I recommend using videos for more complex processes, like giving an overview of the organization of the course for students. I also like videos for laboratory activities, since you can demonstrate how to use equipment, caution students about safety, and give students a heads-up about difficult techniques. Basically, I create videos for processes specific to my course, and use written tutorials for simpler tasks within the LMS. In the next sections, we'll discuss tips for different types of orientations, and what format would work best for each.

Orientation to the Learning Management System

To be successful in your online course, students need to know how to navigate the learning management system (LMS) and the course material, just like you will. I always include a short screencast video showing students where to find everything and how to access materials.

A video orientation to your LMS course will greatly reduce student frustration and questions, since it shows students how to access the major items in the course. You shouldn't try to include everything in this video, or it might be too long to keep students engaged. Just give them enough information to get them started. Here are suggested topics to include in the Orientation Video.

- Where to find the syllabus and how to access it

- Where to find your information so they can contact you

- Where to begin in the course

- How to access the materials

- Where to get help

You will likely need to make other tutorials and/or videos for other places in the course. For example, students who have never taken an online class won't know how to participate in a discussion forum. For the first discussion, you may want to create a video explaining your expectations regarding content for your course. You may use a written tutorial to explain how to access the discussion and reply to other students' posts. In subsequent discussions, you can remind students that the video and tutorial can be found with the first discussion, in case they have forgotten anything. You'll end up having "breadcrumbs" of information periodically throughout your course so that students can find their way.

To save time and energy, take advantage of the tutorials published by your learning management system. They may already have videos or step by step instructions with screenshots to demonstrate how to perform certain tasks. For example, Blackboard has a YouTube channel with videos to help students and instructors learn how to operate within their LMS. The videos show where to find course tools, like email, and how to use the tool. Blackboard offers written tutorials as well, that are supplemented with sample screenshots. You may have to search for the specific tutorial you need, but the search will take less time than creating all the tutorials yourself. Your time is better spent making videos and tutorials that are specific to the content and design in your course, rather than recreating general LMS tutorials.

Below, I have included web addresses for the support areas of several learning management systems, so you can quickly find tutorials to help students in your courses:

1. **Blackboard**

https://help.blackboard.com/

https://www.youtube.com/user/BlackboardTV

2. **Brightspace by Desire2Learn**

https://documentation.brightspace.com/EN/le/-/all/le_intro.htm

https://www.youtube.com/channel/UCLSxTdOzKAFOCZjX-av1aCRQ

3. **Canvas**

https://community.canvaslms.com/community/answers/guides/canvas-guide/getting-started/

https://community.canvaslms.com/community/answers/guides/video-guide

4. **Moodle**

https://docs.moodle.org/33/en/Moodle_video_tutorials

5. **Schoology**

https://support.schoology.com/hc/en-us/sections/200216633-Schoology-Videos

You'll want to make these tutorials easy to access for students, so consider creating a direct link to them from your course homepage.

Orienting Students to the Course Content

Orienting students to the course content involves letting them know what they can expect to learn. You've already written course and lesson objectives (Chapter 7), but students will need to know how use the lesson objectives to get the most out of the lessons. How should students progress through the lessons? How should students study for exams? Offering a brief introduction to each lesson to explain how the lesson relates to the course objectives can help students see the relevance of the lesson. You can highlight important points, clear up misconceptions, and answer anticipated student questions. Students don't always like to read instructions, and sometimes won't understand the written instructions, so a quick video can help them understand what to do.

Labs can be frightening to an online student, since there is no instructor there to guide them through the process. However, emphasizing the process, how the lab connects to the material, and aids understanding can help. A video explaining how labs will be done in your online course can ease student anxiety by ensuring students that you will be available to help. I like to make a specific, short video for each lab, outlining safety precautions and any stumbling blocks students might encounter. In face-to-face classes, I demonstrate how to use certain equipment, like micropipettes. There are written instructions, but I have found that when students see it done, they understand better.

I have to caution you here. It could be tempting to search YouTube for videos about your course content rather than creating your own. You may find videos that are on point and closed-captioned already, and that's great. However, if all of your videos come from outside sources, students may question who is actually teaching the course. I have had students tell me that in another biology course, all of the videos were taken from YouTube, and the students felt like the teacher was not really teaching. Again, the personal touch is important in online classes, so students know who you are, and that you care about their learning.

Safety Orientation

Since we teach science laboratory courses, we must include safety information for our students. Failing to discuss, model, and require safety procedures can lead to accidents, injury, and perhaps even legal action. Students must understand that, even though they will be using small amounts of chemicals, accidents can still happen. Even if they are utilizing a computer simulation or remote lab, students must understand safety precautions and procedures for future reference. For my face-to-face classes, my students complete a safety activity and sign and submit a safety contract. Students in my online classes complete the same requirements before they are allowed to access any other lessons.

The first assignment students complete is a game in which they must perform basic laboratory safety tasks. At the end of the game, students receive a certificate of completion, and they upload that to a dropbox in the LMS for a grade. Students get a review over lab safety, and learn how to take a screenshot and upload files at the same time (if they didn't know already).

I then have students watch a video that is specific to the course and the types of labs they will be doing. This is an important step, since it informs students of specific safety precautions and lets students know that you care about their safety. For my safety video, I put on my safety goggles, my apron, and gloves, and prepare the area like students should. I like to keep the video upbeat, so that students will watch the entire video. Below is a list of talking points for your safety video:

- **Personal Protection Equipment**—I recommend you have all the safety equipment you want students to use with you when you make the video so that students can see exactly what you mean when you discuss types of personal protective equipment. For example, students may not understand the distinction between safety glasses and safety goggles, but having the correct eye protection can save their eyesight.

- **Student Laboratory Space**—Since students will be completing labs at their home or dorm room, it is important that students understand the amount and type of space that they will need. For many students, this area will be the kitchen. Remind students to clear the counter area of all food-related materials, like small appliances, canisters, etc. Also remind them to clean up the area thoroughly when they are finished with a lab, and some suggestions about what to use to clean up will likely prevent student questions.

- **Food and Drink**—Since students will be at home, possibly in the kitchen, when they are completing labs, they will have access to food and drink. Remind students to not eat, drink, or chew gum while they are performing laboratory activities, and why this is important.

- **Friends, children, spouses, dogs, cats, etc.**—I have a dog who likes to cruise for crumbs in the kitchen. There have been several times when I have almost tripped over him. I would hate for him (or me) to get injured because I was doing a lab in my kitchen and spilled a chemical. I tell students this, and even show them my dog in the video. Students need to keep their pets, children, little brothers/sisters, spouses, friends, weird cousins, unwelcome neighbors, boyfriends/girlfriends, aunts, uncles, anyone and anything else out of harm's way.

Finally, I have students read and sign a safety contract that I modified from one I use in my face-to-face classes. I tell students to print the safety contract, sign it, and scan it. Since it is the first file students will download in the course, I create a tutorial explaining how to download and print the file. Students then must upload the scanned file to a dropbox in the LMS. I refer students to the tutorial I used with the Safety Activity Certificate of Completion if they forget how to upload the file. Once they have uploaded the safety contract, the rest of the material for the first week appears. Alternatively, you could include the safety information as part of the syllabus, and have students sign a statement saying they agree to all terms (including the safety contract) in the syllabus. I prefer to leave it as a separate file so students concentrate on the safety information as they begin working in the course. I have included a sample online laboratory safety contract.

Figure 10.2A – Sample Online Lab Safety Agreement

Students must abide by the following safety rules at all times while performing activities for class.

1. Read and follow all instructions for completing laboratory activities.

2. Ask questions about anything you do not understand before completing the activity.

3. Proceed with caution when completing laboratory and field activities for class.

4. Only students enrolled in the laboratory course can perform course activities.

5. Keep pets, children or other family members, and friends away from laboratory materials at all times.

6. Long hair, dangling jewelry, bracelets or loose clothing should be confined while performing laboratory activities. You should wear clothing that covers your skin as much as possible when using chemicals.

7. Do not eat, drink, smoke or apply cosmetics while performing laboratory activities.

8. Keep laboratory materials away from sources of food and drink.

9. Safety goggles/glasses must be worn when working with preserved specimens, when using hazardous chemicals, when glassware and solutions are heated, and as directed by lab instructor. Contact lenses should not be worn while performing laboratory activities.

10. Chemicals are never to be smelled or tasted.

11. Unauthorized experiments are NOT allowed.

12. Take care around glassware to avoid cutting yourself or others. Follow laboratory directions with regard to proper disposal of materials.

13. Protective gloves must be worn as directed in the laboratory instructions.

14. Bandage any cuts on hands before dissecting or using chemical reagents. Use care when working with scalpels and other sharp instruments.

15. Keep your laboratory work area as uncluttered as possible.

16. Clean all materials thoroughly after completing the laboratory activity.

17. Wash your hands after completing the laboratory activity.

18. USE COMMON SENSE!!

NOTE: If you have a health condition that would make you especially susceptible to chemicals used in the laboratory for this course, you MUST advise your lab instructor so that your safety can be given appropriate consideration.

I (print name) _____have thoroughly read and understand this safety agreement.

I understand all the rules, and I will observe them throughout the semester.

If I have a question regarding safety or experimental procedures, I will ask the instructor for further explanation before proceeding.

Signed: _____

Date: _____

CHAPTER 11
BUILDING A COMMUNITY OF LEARNERS

11.1 Communicating With Your Students

The First Principle of Good Practice in Undergraduate Education encourages contact between students and faculty (Chickering and Gamson, 1987). You can't greet online students at the door, shake their hands or ask them how things are going, but as an instructor who wants to have your students succeed, you must let students know you are there to support them. Contact students who don't log in for several days and/or miss deadlines. And don't just try once. Keep trying. Once you contact them, make a plan to ensure the student does not get further behind.

In online courses you must pay special attention to maintaining contact with students, getting to know your students, and letting them get to know you. In your communications to students, give examples from your life that relate to course content. Let students see you as a regular person, who teaches and has hobbies and family responsibilities. I record audio and video for my students, even though I don't like hearing my voice and seeing myself on the recording. In some of the videos, the phone will ring or my dog will bark. It's always amusing to me when students comment about how many times the phone rang or ask what kind of dog I have. I know then that they viewed the recording. I could go back and do the recording again or edit the recording to take out those interruptions, but the recordings will never be perfect, and the imperfections are part of what make me human and relatable to my students. You want students to feel as though they can talk to you, ask you questions, and view you as a real person rather than just some abstract image out in cyberspace.

Since you won't see the students in class each week, you have to design a system of contacting them, explaining what they need to do for each assignment, reminding them of due dates, and giving them feedback. I make a habit of posting a weekly announcement with the week's calendar. I point out any modifications that have been made to the calendar, remind students of upcoming deadlines, and give tips about tasks that will take more time than others. You can send a video or audio file by email or post it to the announcement page so students can see and hear you discuss these things.

I took an online graduate class a while back, and emailed the instructor a question because there was a discrepancy between instructions in the syllabus versus the instructions posted to the LMS. I received a response, but it was not from the instructor. It was from his graduate teaching assistant. Look, we're all busy, and he's lucky to have an assistant. There are many days I wish I had one. However, receiving the reply from the assistant made me feel like the instructor was, at best, too busy to answer my email. I hoped it was not because he didn't care to answer my email, but the thought did cross my mind.

Contact with students must be early and frequent, and one way to implement this is to call every student enrolled in the course at the start of the semester (Angelino, Williams and Natvig, 2007). I have found that this type of personal communication, while time-consuming, can benefit students greatly. I had a student in an on-line class who did not log in on the first day of the course. I tried emailing him, with no success. After the third day of the course, I called and left a message. The next day I received an email from the student explaining that he required accommodations, and had the letter from the Office of Disabilities, but could not figure out how to get it to me since he did not live near campus. After arranging for electronic submission of documents, I made the necessary accommodations to his assignments in the LMS, and he completed the course successfully. In retrospect, I wish I had tried calling him sooner so he would not have lost those four days of work time in the course. Of course, calling a student via telephone is not the only method that can be used for student contact. Skype, Facetime, and online office hours allow you to interact with students in real time as well. See Section 11.6 on Communication tools.

11.2 Learning Communities

In online classes, there are no hallways in which students can stop and chat with you, asking whatever questions might pop into their heads. There is no time before or after class in which students will hang around with each other to discuss school, work, or the latest movie. How do you create a community in your classroom when students never physically see each other or you?

We have already discussed the need for constant communication, but learning communities are built on more than just instructor-student communication. Students need to meet their classmates, discuss assignments, ask questions, or form study groups. Student interaction helps create an engaging learning environment (Ter-Stephanian, 2012), and diversity in the student population can provide a potential for multi-cultural learning (Hunter and Austin, 2015).

Four elements of online learning communities exist: community, learning, network, and technology (Office of Learning Technologies, 1998). Community develops through interaction around common interests, and learning occurs on the member and the community level. Networks within learning communities allow members to easily share knowledge and resources, and technology facilitates this process (Tu and Corry, 2002).

In a survey by the EDUCAUSE Center for Applied Research, most students agreed or strongly agreed that technology helps them engage and build professional relationships with other students. Some students (38 percent) also indicated that technology also helped them develop personal relationships with other students (Brooks, 2016). Figure 11.2A summarizes how students have used technology in their courses.

Figure 11.2A – Student Technology Efficacy, adapted from Figure 15, Student Technology Efficacy, D. Christopher Brooks, ECAR Study of Undergraduate Students and Information Technology, 2016, p. 29, https://library.educause.edu/~/media/files/library/2016/10/ers1605.pdf.

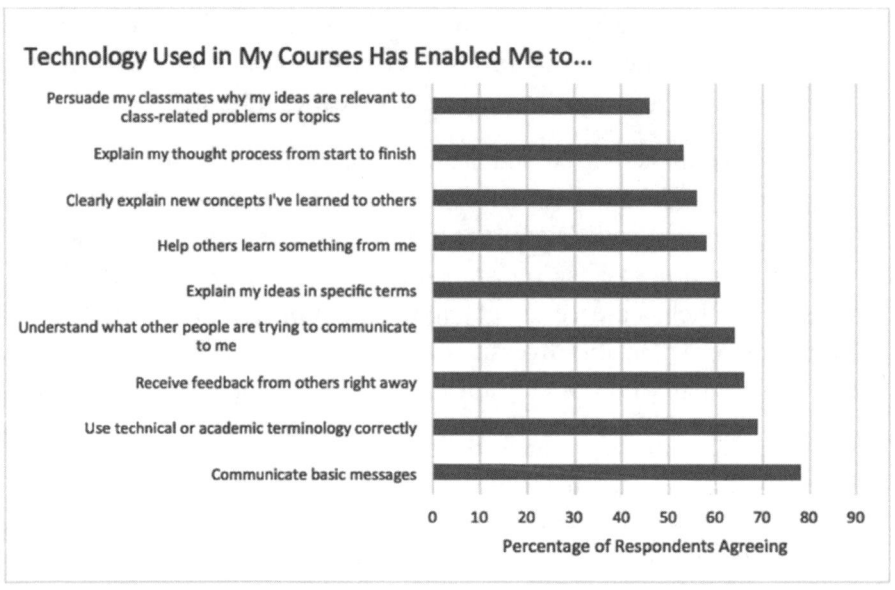

Students use technology to facilitate communication, which is a necessity in a learning community. Students also seem to appreciate prompt feedback (the Fourth Principle of Good Practice – Chickering and Gamson, 1987), since they have ranked this as the third most common use of technology. Other items noted by students involve explaining their ideas and understanding the ideas of others. In online classes, instructors must optimize the use of technology to facilitate student interaction and formation of a learning community.

Google Docs, wikis, blogs, and Twitter have been shown to provide students with a sense of belonging in a learning community. Exchanging comments on wikis and blogs allows students to actively discuss ideas and perspectives, contributing to the sense of community. Receiving feedback from other students about class work can support the formation of a learning community, as well. (Abdelmalak, 2015).

11.3 Discussion Forums

In Chapter 7, discussions are included as part of lessons so that students could construct knowledge collaboratively. Discussion forums can also assist in developing a learning community, and enhance feelings of satisfaction with a course (Wilson, Codry and King, 2004). Students need a place to ask each other questions that are not necessarily on topic. For this reason, many instructors include a discussion board, Watercooler Discussions, or Off-topic Discussions.

Instructions state that posts are not required, but students can ask questions, let people know about an activity, or ask for recommendations about future classes. Sometimes there will be few posts, but other times there could be many. One instructor reported that students with common problems shared moral support, helping to create a sense of community (Ter-Stephanian, 2012).

11.4 Social Media

Can we get away from social media these days? It's highly unlikely, so we might as well embrace it and make the most of it. Social media can focus people on what they have in common, drawing them together from all over the globe. Students can use social media to find their similarities, but also explore their differences (Hunter and Austin, 2015). Instructor involvement is vital to maintaining learning communities created via social media (de Lima and Zorrilla, 2017).

Social media helps you and your students connect outside of the "classroom." I give students my Twitter handle, and tell them that I post about teaching, educational technology, science, and student accomplishments. I post pictures of graduations, awards, and research done by students, create hashtags for classes and topics so students can find the Tweets. Students don't have to follow me or give me their Twitter handles (though several do).

Facebook has been used in classes to develop learning communities in which students communicated and collaborated to solve problems and connect emotionally. Students reassured each other, offered assistance and appreciation, and discovered commonalities with each other (Whittaker, Howarth and Lymn, 2014). Most students are familiar with how to use Facebook, and that could help make it a valuable means of communication between students in online classes.

Your students will also use the latest social media platforms. Don't feel pressured to join and post to all forms of social media. Let students know that they have the option to email each other using the LMS tools, and that via email they can exchange social media or other contact information. One of the students could set up a Facebook page or develop a class hashtag. Students just need to know how to first contact each other to get the ball rolling.

11.5 Facilitation of Student Collaboration

Students don't have to be in the same location to work cooperatively to complete projects or assignments. Google has several applications that allow shared editing, and I was surprised to learn two years ago that some of my students had never used Google applications (other than the search engine). Those students appreciated the fact that they could work in the same file independently and form one cohesive document. A few said they took the collaboration one step further by talking on the phone and discussing edits as they were being made.

It is helpful to outline expectations of behavior in group collaboration, since certain behaviors can affect how well each group works together and the quality of the product. For example, group members should offer encouragement, appreciation, and congratulations on a job well done. They need to take and give feedback seriously, since it is a way for them to learn how to improve. Groups should decide how to resolve potential conflicts and how each member will contribute to the group project. The quality of group projects is clearly correlated to the amount of collaboration within groups (Thompson and Ku, 2006), so helping students understand how to collaborate in online classes can help them greatly.

A valid concern from students and instructors is the potential lack of student participation in groups (loafing). How do you know if a student is loafing and letting his or her partners do all of the work? One way to help delineate which group member completed which tasks is to require that students use tools within the LMS to communicate. This allows instructors to see how well the group communicates and which students may be participating more than others (Morgan, et al., 2014). If the product is a written assignment, groups can use Google Docs to collaborate. Google Docs tracks changes, and instructors can require students to share the file with them so they can view who completed what part of the document. Also, no one can permanently delete material from the file, since you can restore previous versions.

If a problem arises, or instructors need to meet with groups for another reason, they can use Zoom, Blackboard Collaborate, or other synchronous online meeting software. Since most of these software applications have breakout rooms, these can be used to allow groups to meet virtually online to share ideas, discuss completed work, and meet with the instructor (Nehme, 2008).

Requiring student-to-student collaboration creates a community of learners. You can do this by posting discussion boards on course topics throughout the semester. Assigning a participation grade can help ensure all students post their thoughts.

11.6 Communication Tools

Instructor/student communication and student/student communication is vital to the success in online courses, which is likely why Chickering and Gamson included contact between instructors and students as their First Principle of Good Practice (1987). You should decide which communication tools you will use to facilitate that communication in your course. Students will not be familiar with every form of communication available, so once you decide which ones to use, give students an overview of how to use them.

- **Email** – You may think students are familiar with email, but it never hurts to discuss its proper use with students. You'll likely find that students are not accustomed to using their college email, even though that is how the college communicates with them. Most colleges frown upon using other email accounts to communicate with students due to privacy issues, so make sure students know how to contact tech support if they need help with accessing their college email or setting it up on their phones. Having the college email on their phones increases student use of that email.

- **Skype** – Skype is a free online communication tool that allows voice and video calls. You can set up appointments with students and answer their questions face to face.

- **Google Hangouts** – Google Hangouts is much like Skype, with the exception that with Hangouts, you can schedule multiple students together, like you might with office hours or tutoring sessions.

- **Zoom** – Zoom is an online meeting tool that allows you to share your desktop. I have access to Zoom through McLennan Community College currently, and I like it because it is more like an online classroom in which I can show students what I'm typing or otherwise doing on my laptop. It's great for those times when students are having issues with technology. Contact your college's IT department to see if you have access to Zoom, and how to use it.

- **Blackboard Collaborate** – Much like Zoom, Blackboard Collaborate allows online meeting attendees to share information in virtual meetings. Contact your college's IT department to see if you have access to Collaborate, and how to use it.

- **Remind** – Remind is a free online text messaging platform. Students love texting, so Remind is a terrific way to send reminders to students of upcoming due dates. You can set up messages in advance, so you don't have to worry about forgetting when times get busy. You can set up messages from your computer, phone, or tablet, which makes it very versatile.

Planning for student engagement, maintaining contact with students, and building a community of learners does much more than keep students in your course. Over the years, I have learned about my students, their families, their jobs, their struggles, and their successes. I am always amazed at what students tell me during a semester, and thankful that some have chosen to remain in contact even after several years. I have seen graduations, new jobs, weddings, and even births. Some I witnessed in person, but many I witness online. Either way, it brings me joy to see my former students growing their careers and families.

CHAPTER 12
STRATEGIES FOR ONLINE STUDENT SUCCESS & COURSE COMPLETION

12.1 Retaining Your Online Students

Retention of students in academic programs is one measure of teaching effectiveness in online courses. In a study of community college students, those who took some courses online showed higher retention rates than those who took no courses online. However, students who took all of their courses online were more likely to drop out of courses than those who took no courses online (Scott, Swan and Daston, 2016).

Unfortunately, this seems to be a trend, since online classes have historically shown higher dropout rates than face-to-face classes (Hiltz, 1997). A study from the University of Illinois at Urbana-Champaign found that students are most likely to drop out of a program after only a few courses, with those who complete more courses being more likely to finish the entire program (Willging and Johnson, 2009). This is not surprising, considering that students who struggle with adapting to online course delivery and/or technology can become frustrated and drop out before they have invested more time, effort, and money. Once a student has become invested in a program, they are more likely to complete it (Willging and Johnson, 2009). This suggests that, while it is important to design any course well, if you teach an introductory level course, you must pay very close attention to organization, ease of use, and helping students adapt to online learning.

To better engage and retain students, Strandberg and Campbell recommend the following (2014):

- Create opportunities for students to get to know at least two other students. This relates directly to the second Principle of Good Practice, and encourages group collaboration and discussions.

- Provide current, real-world examples that relate to course material. Providing relevancy for your adult students ties into their need to know, readiness to learn, and orientation to learn. Students can apply information to their own lives and what is happening around them.

- Break up readings with purposeful visuals. Too much all at once can lower student attention, so add some videos and images.

- Communicate with students several times a week. Refer to the First Principle of Good Practice. Ensure students know that you are there for them when they need you, and don't wait for them to contact you. Reach out to your students.

Understanding Student Procrastination

Students in all courses procrastinate, but the extent and effects of procrastination in online classes can be greater than in face-to-face classes. One reason for this lies in the nature of the online course itself: flexibility. With no strict weekly schedule, the opportunities for procrastination are greater. Students in face-to-face classes are exposed to the material on a regular basis by attending class at specific times each week. Even if those students put off studying until right before the exam, they have at least spent some time with the material on a regular basis.

Occasionally, you'll have a student contact you because they are not doing as well as they would like in the course (usually right after an exam). It's pretty obvious why a student isn't doing well if they have not submitted assignments, but what if they have submitted everything? This is where the LMS data comes in handy. I typically schedule a live meeting for questions like this, and I prepare for the meeting my looking at the student's data. I look to see how long the student took to take exams and quizzes, how many times the student logs in per week on average, and the average amount of time spent per session. I build my courses so that most of the material is completed within the LMS, so data is pretty accurate about time spent. In many situations, the student is not spending a lot of time in the course compared to other students who perform better, and I tell this to the student. Over time, record the average participation times and correlate that data to grades. Share that information with your students: "Students who make a grade of A spend an average of _____ hours per week interacting with the course material."

You can use LMS log-in reports to determine the most common times students in your course are logging in to the LMS during the semester. If you want to schedule a live session for discussion, review, or tutorials, the reports would show the optimal day and time combinations. Different learning management systems will have different reports available, but these are two that are fairly common.

A student (let's call him Robert) is enrolled in an English class during a fall semester. All assignments, quizzes, and tests are due by the end of the semester. He procrastinates until Thanksgiving break, and plans to complete the entire course that week. While Robert does complete the course, he reports not liking the course. This correlates with research into procrastination in online courses. Procrastination is tied to dissatisfaction with the course itself (Elvers, Polzella and Graetz, 2003).

Robert also suggests that he probably did not do as well in that course as he could have, if he had not procrastinated as much. This correlates with research on student procrastination, since students who procrastinate in online courses typically earn lower exam scores.

Reducing procrastination in our classes will help improve student performance and satisfaction, so, online instructors must create a learning environment which discourages procrastination. We will discuss several strategies to discourage procrastination in the following sections of this chapter.

Frequent, Consistent Deadlines

We'll start with the simplest strategy to implement: frequent, consistent deadlines. You should have built deadlines into your course calendar, so you're already on your way to limiting procrastination. However, you still must support students while they are adapting to the course deadlines, since not all of your students will demonstrate the same readiness to learn. I suggest to my students that they put upcoming deadline reminders in their phones. However, we must be careful here to emphasize that a reminder right before the deadline won't help. Encourage students to set a study schedule and put those study times in their phones. Basically, it is like they are setting their own class times. When they do this, they are less likely miss course deadlines.

You must be prepared for those students who don't complete tasks on time. I tend to allow students an exemption from the late work policy, though I don't advertise this. I have found that conscientious students will email me when they realize they missed a deadline, explain why, and ask for assistance and understanding. I usually allow the exception once for everyone who does this, because I am more interested in seeing whether they have mastered the material than never allowing them to correct their mistake.

12.2 Student Needs and Motivation

Online classes require that students be self-motivated. That's why I include that statement in my Welcome Email before classes start. If we can help students understand and internalize their motivation, they will be more likely to succeed in their courses. Before we can begin to address student motivation, we must address student needs. How can a student do well in a class if they don't have enough to eat?

 For online students, knowing their needs and how to help can be difficult. However, we can ensure that students know that they can contact us for help and know where else to go for help. Post announcements and/or email students with information about services available to them (Battista and Ruble, 2014).

We have already discussed including information about student resources in the syllabus and links to student resources in the LMS. However, simply having a list does not ensure students will read the information or utilize the services. Remind students of the services available periodically during the semester. Some colleges offer online tutoring, food banks, and/or counseling services. Acknowledging that our students face challenges outside of school that can affect their school life makes students feel like they are not alone in their struggles, and can help them feel more comfortable asking for help. A "Did You Know?" email or announcement can remind students about services available to them through the college.

Once we do what we can to help fill students' needs, we can begin to address what motivates our students. Adult students will have different types and amounts of motivation. Some may show some intrinsic motivation, which results from finding a task interesting and/or enjoyable. Much emphasis has been placed on intrinsic motivation since it results in deep learning and creative thinking (Ryan and Deci, 2000), and instructors must strive to incorporate activities that are interesting and enjoyable for students. How instructors present course content to their students can address different types of motivation. Strive to increase intrinsic motivation in your students by incorporating a variety of activities that generate interest and enjoyment.

In Chapter 7, we discussed the importance of designing engaging lessons through authentic learning experiences such as simulations and real-world applications. Rich visual aids like video, virtual field trips or even real field activities can spark curiosity and interest. You can even schedule virtual meetings with experts to discuss current research and applications. All of this can help spark intrinsic motivation in your students (Battista and Ruble, 2014).

 Encourage students to develop and share their learning goals and reasons for taking the course (Battista and Ruble, 2014).

The Sixth Principle of Good Practice encourages high expectations (Chickering and Gamson, 1987). An expectation of success can become a self-fulfilling prophecy, since students are more likely to work harder and be more persistent. Correspondingly, if students believe they have the ability to do well (self-efficacy), they are more likely to do so. Instructors can help increase students self-efficacy by assisting students in setting short-term and long-term mastery goals. Often, students set performance goals (i.e. to earn a certain grade or to not look stupid in front of the teacher or classmates), but these types of goals are less likely to consistently lead to positive outcomes. If students set goals to improve their abilities, to master certain knowledge and/or skills, the student begins to worry less about external grades or what others think about them. They concern themselves more with monitoring their own progress, which can increase persistence and the likelihood of reaching their short- and long-term goals (National Academy of Sciences, 2012).

It's important to determine why students are enrolled in your class so that you can know how to help drive students to be successful. Volunteering information about yourself will make students feel more comfortable with you and your course. Usually, a few students will respond, whether in the discussion forum or via email. My students have told me that they are glad I understand how difficult it is to return to college as a nontraditional student. Sometimes students feel like we (teachers) can't understand the problems they face, so the more we can demonstrate that we are there to help them, the better.

 Emphasize how the class content and activities are relevant to students' future careers (Battista and Ruble, 2014).

As you facilitate your course, look back at the answers to your "Icebreaker Discussion" and consider your students' career choices so you can better address each student's need to know and orientation to learning. A student who is taking a class because it can help her/him advance in a career is showing extrinsic motivation. Instructors can build on this by relating how the activities in the class can apply to a student's chosen career path. For example, students who want to be teachers could benefit from understanding why you have chosen certain instructional strategies. Students who wish to work in a laboratory will directly benefit from the laboratory activities. Pointing this out to students can help them accept and understand the importance of doing their best on the tasks.

Adult learners will vary in their need to know and orientation to learning (Conaway and Zorn-Arnold, 2015), but one thing remains constant. When students don't understand why they are performing certain tasks and assignments, they can become less motivated to complete them and less engaged in the course. Students in your classes may not come right out and ask you why they need to learn this, or why they must work in groups, but they could still be thinking it. Giving a brief explanation of how the tasks relates to future classes or future career choices can help students connect with the course material. Ask yourself these questions so you'll be prepared to answer them (Egbert and Roe, 2014). If you can't figure out how it relates to students' lives and/or careers, perhaps it is time to rethink that activity.

CHAPTER 13
ASSESSMENTS

13.1 Formative Assessments

To be an effective instructor, you must consistently assess your students' learning. In the 5E instructional model, formative assessments occur throughout the Engage, Explore, Explain, and Elaborate stages (Bybee, 2014) [see Chapter 7]. Formative assessments provide feedback and high expectations for students, two of the Principles of Good Practice (Chickering and Gamson, 1987).

 Use formative assessments to determine how students are progressing toward the learning objectives, and to give students feedback to help them master the course material.

Formative assessments are more about the learning process than the grade. They provide instructors with information which can be used to adjust instruction and help students master the material. In turn, instructors give students feedback about their learning and how to improve (Myers, 2015). For example, you can use a pre-assessment in your classes to determine your students' prior knowledge and determine areas in which students are strong or weak. Students should not earn a grade for the pre-assessment. Then, as you teach, administer formative assessments to analyze student response and give students feedback. Feedback is vital to the process of learning, so students know where to focus and can move further and faster toward mastery. Assessments without feedback and an opportunity to improve are not formative. The Unit Assessment Cycle (figure 13.1A) is one example of how instructors can incorporate formative assessments into a unit of instruction.

Figure 13.1A – The Unit Assessment Cycle

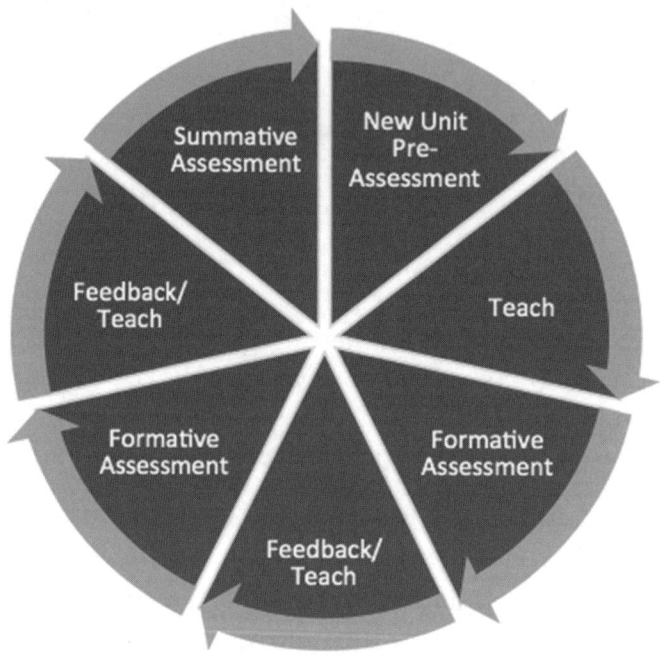

In the unit assessment cycle, each unit begins with a pre-assessment, so the instructor has data to guide instruction. Students progress through instructional activities and complete the first formative assessment. You analyze the assessment and provide specific feedback to each student. Students use the feedback to improve, and continue with instructional activities until they reach the next formative assessment. The cycle continues until the summative assessment, which is a final chance for students to demonstrate mastery of the material. The next unit would begin with the next pre-assessment.

 Your students may not understand the purpose of the pre-assessment, and worry because they do not know the answers. Make sure to explain the purpose of the pre-assessment, so that students understand its role in their learning.

I tell students that online quizzes are a way for me to get them to look at the material and then get an idea of how well they understand the material. I know what you're thinking... How do I keep students from cheating on these quizzes? For the online quizzes, I want students to use their notes and other materials to help them on the questions they don't know. I want them to ask each other questions and help each other understand. I want them to contact me about anything they don't understand. I want them to do these things to help increase their understanding and mastery of the material, so I don't consider any of these things, when done for these online quizzes, as cheating. Once students understand that the quizzes are part of their learning process, they use them as intended. (For the most part – there's always one or two who don't use the process to improve their learning.)

 Students sometimes only want to complete tasks that are graded. Even though I use online quizzes as formative assessments, the online quizzes have a grade associated with them to encourage participation. Consider having your formative assessments (quizzes, discussions, etc.) as a category worth a small amount of the course average (5-10 percent), so that students will complete them.

Writing assignments may also be used as formative assessments. If you assign students an essay or paper, have periodic deadlines for portions of the assessment rather than just the final due date. For example, you could have students submit two sources they would like to use and why. You can give students feedback about reliable sources and proper citations.

Online students may not be aware of the institutional learning resources available to them. Check with your college to determine what services are available to students and how students access those services. Then, build in progress checks or extra points to encourage students to take advantage of these services.

If your college has a writing center or tutors available to students online, this is a wonderful option! Require that students submit a draft of their paper to a tutor provided by the college (often they can do this by email through the college writing center or academic assistance) for feedback. Students can get help without going to campus, and you don't have to look over all your students' rough drafts!

Each of these ideas may be only a few points toward a student's final grade on the writing assignment, but it will encourage students to make timely progress on their papers, and get students the help they need. I had one student refer to the Writing Center at my college as a magical place where homework gets done.

The following unique formative assessment tools can be used in face-to-face and online courses. Each tool can be easily adapted to different science disciplines and course topics, and students enjoy the gaming aspect of the tools. Each has pre-made games that you can adapt and use, or you can create your own games.

GooseChase – **GooseChase (www.goosechase.com/edu)** is an online scavenger hunt platform, and it's a way to gamify education. Sign up for an educator account, create a game and students complete challenges within the game to earn points. I've used it for extra credit, for a review, and as a way for students to demonstrate real-world application of knowledge. For example, we covered types of plants, and I created a GooseChase for students to use outside of class time, wherever they were, to find diverse types of plants in the environment. I could have had students do this as a report, but formatting the "homework" as a scavenger hunt made it more fun for the students. Students became competitive and tried to find plants that others had not found, and tried to find more examples than other students. Suddenly, what could have been a boring virtual plant collection turned into an engaging game. Students can collaborate on games and their points aggregate automatically, and there's even a feature that allows instructors to share games.

BreakoutEdu Digital – **BreakoutEdu Digital** games provide another way to gamify your lessons. Students must use critical thinking skills to solve puzzles and find solutions to digital "locks." Each game centers around a problem, and there are several games available that others have made for classes. This makes a great review game, or you could introduce the Breakout game at the beginning of a unit as an Engage or Explore activity. You can create your own games using Google Sites as well, or pay for access to BreakoutEdu's Platform, which provides access to other games and software to create digital games.

Remember, assessments are not formative without feedback, so refer to the appropriate sections of this book more information on planning for student feedback.

13.2 Laboratory Assessments

Think about the lab activities you chose in Chapter 5. If you chose a lab kit or online access to a program of virtual labs, there may be pre-made assessments. Measure lab skills using formative assessments. You are free to use prebuilt assessments, but create some of your own as well. If you are writing your own labs, you'll need to write your own assessments to match. How?

Think about what students do in a face-to-face lab. Do they write lab reports? Do they take quizzes over the material? Your online students can do those as well, but there's one more layer of assessment in an online lab class. When students are in the lab with you doing the lab activities, they can ask questions and you can monitor their progress. How can that happen in an online class? A virtual lab system can keep a record of everything a student does in the lab so instructors can monitor student progress. For labs that students are supposed to perform in the real world, you can have students take pictures of their process and/or results to include in the lab report. Afraid they will share pictures or steal them from the Internet? Have students include their college identification card or other form of ID in the picture.

For example, I want students to look at the world around them in my biology classes. I have a Nature Selfie assignment in which students find a park or other natural area and take two pictures: one of the ecosystem, and a selfie with the ecosystem in the background. The selfie is so that I know they went there to take the picture and didn't borrow one from somewhere. The other photo shows an uninterrupted view of the ecosystem so that students can describe various aspects of it by referring to the picture. Both assignments ask students to apply knowledge they have gained to the real world around them. I have included instructions for my Nature Selfie assignment below.

Figure 13.2A - Levels of Organization & Diversity of Life Assignment: Nature Selfie!

Part 1:

1. Go to a state park or other natural area. Your yard does not count. The area should include multiple types of organisms and habitats.

2. Once there, you will take two pictures for your assignment: a picture of the area that shows the general location, and another that is a selfie of yourself in the same area.

Part 2:

1. Once you have your pictures, you will identify the biological organization shown in your ecosystem picture. You must identify at least 5 levels of biological organization shown in the picture, and explain your reasoning in at least two complete sentences for each biological level (10 total sentences minimum).

2. You must use correct grammar and spelling in your explanation.

3. Make sure that I can tell which part of your picture corresponds to which level of biological organization.

Part 3:

1. Pick one organism shown in your picture, and do research to find its Domain, Kingdom, Phylum and Class. Use the chart in this Learning Module. You can also use http://www.itis.gov if you know what kind of organism it is, or do a Google search for the classification.

2. Make sure to use reliable sources (No Wikipedia, About.com, Blogs, etc.). If you have questions about what a reliable source is, please visit this website: http://www.library.georgetown.

---

edu/tutorials/research-guides/evaluating-Internet-content, or just email me and ask. If in doubt, you should probably find another source.

3. Identify the organism in the picture, and make sure that the organism can be seen in the picture.

4. The format you choose to use is completely up to you. If you enjoy making videos, go for it! If you are proficient in PowerPoint, use it! If you want to use Word, that's acceptable too!

5. When you are finished with your assignment, export it into a PDF format before you upload it to ensure it will open correctly for me. Other files types may not work, which means you would not get a grade (0).

Please see the photo below and on the next page which illustrate how an instructor could highlight portions of her/his picture.

Part 1: Here are my pictures from a local natural area. The first picture on the previous page is my selfie, and the second picture, above, is zoomed in to show more detail.

Part 2: The turtles or trees can represent one level of biological organization. The pond can represent another. (I'm not telling you which or why – that's your job for your picture!)

Part 3: Refer to the turtles highlighted in the picture. (You need to do the research to identify domain, kingdom, phylum, and class.)

Anything you would normally have your students complete on paper will need to be changed in format since you won't be using paper in your course. You can build quizzes and tests in the LMS and students can take them online. A student can write a lab report, include text, graphs, and pictures in the file, and upload the file to a dropbox in the LMS. Students can even upload videos.

Assessing lab skills is a challenge all science instructors must tackle, whether students are in the lab with the instructor or not. Labeling equipment and explaining its use, or identifying tissue types or cell structures from images is fairly common, but these examples do not allow the instructor to directly assess a student's ability to use equipment (Anderson, 2017). We can assess student lab skills when we watch them perform lab activities, but how can we assess this in online classes when we aren't even in the same room with them while they are performing the laboratory activities?

Certainly, this question would be even more difficult to answer if students were completing cookbook labs with materials found in a kitchen rather than scientific instruments. In simulations, you can view what the students have done and perhaps even have them record their screen while performing certain tasks. This would allow you to view how the students perform with the equipment in the simulations. In face-to-face classes, review and feedback of student recordings of Gram staining procedure significantly improved student performance on their second attempt (Lipson and Gair, 2011). If students are using lab kits, they can record themselves using the equipment or performing a task and submit the video online. In both situations, instructors can give students feedback about technique.

In his microbiology course, Jeff Dykes of Wenatchee Valley College uses what he calls a task book to assess student skills on procedures. The task book is presented to students at the start of each semester, and students are expected to progress through the task book as they progress through the course. Each student demonstrates each skill to the instructor, and if done correctly, the instructor deems that a student proficient at the task. If a student is not proficient, the instructor gives the student feedback so that they can practice correct technique and try again (Dykes, 2012). Allowing students multiple attempts toward mastery turns the task book into a formative assessment. In online classes, students could record themselves performing a task and submit it for review to the instructor. Depending on the number of tasks in the task book and the number of students, viewing and generating feedback could become cumbersome. I would suggest limiting the tasks to the most essential, and having periodic deadlines. For example, if you have 10 essential tasks, you could require submission of at least one new task video per week.

You'll also have to decide whether to grade the skills assessment. Dykes assigned the task book a grade weight equal to approximately 5-10 percent of each student's final average in the course (Dykes, 2012). Another option is for instructors to grant students Digital Badges upon completion of tasks, which represent proficiency at those skills. A digital badge can follow a student beyond the classroom, since it is hosted online and can be displayed on social media sites such as LinkedIn (Hensiek, et al., 2017). The process for students to earn badges would be the same as to complete the task book mentioned above.

13.3 Summative Assessments

The most effective summative assessments begin with the end in mind. Summative assessments occur after students have completed instruction on a topic, like at the end of a unit of material. There is little chance for a student to receive feedback and improve his or her grade after a summative assessment. Summative assessments are an evaluation of learning and mastery of the material (Myers, 2015), and would occur during the Evaluate stage of the 5E Instructional Model (Bybee, 2014).

Often, college instructors write their exams right before they give them in class. For a face-to-face class, this can be beneficial, since an instructor might change their instruction based on the class. In an online course, this is not typically feasible, especially if you have students progressing through the course at different rates. For online classes, all of the exams should be created before the semester begins, and instructors must ensure that lessons provide the instruction needed for students to do well on the exams.

If you have a bank of questions you use for quizzes and tests in your face-to-face course, you can use them in your online course as well. Each LMS has different options for how you have upload questions from document files. One way to set up quizzes and tests in your LMS is to use the test generator software (ExamView, TestGen, etc.) supplied by your textbook publisher.

First, use the test generator to select questions for a unit or chapter. You can select the exact questions you want so that everyone would have the same version of the quiz/test, or you can select a group of questions to use as a bank within your LMS for a quiz/test. It is essential that you take the time to select questions that match your instruction, since test banks will often have a very broad range of questions, including some about topics which you do not cover in your course.

Once you're done selecting questions, save the test file. Then, export the test to a format that works with your LMS. For example, I have used ExamView and TestGen, to export tests as Blackboard compatible files. The precise details depend on both your LMS and your test generator software.

To help prevent cheating, you can upload many questions (a test bank) from each chapter, and have the LMS select questions (per your specifications) at random for each student. For example, in a quiz/test over chapter 1, you might have 25 questions in the bank, but each student would only see 10 in his or her quiz/test. There are other options for preventing academic dishonesty as well, but we'll discuss them in more detail in Chapter 14.

Once you have exported your test/quiz into a format compatible with your LMS, you'll need to upload the questions into your LMS. Again, the exact procedure will depend on your LMS. In Blackboard, you'll enter your course shell and click on Assignment/test. Then, you'll select "upload" to add questions. You can then upload your quiz/test file, so you'll have access to those questions when you build your quiz/test in the course. The important thing for you to do here is to create the quizzes and tests you'll need for your course.

Most instructors think of tests when they hear the term summative assessment, but there are other options. A student could complete a project that demonstrates skill and knowledge of the material as well. For example, a student could create a Rube-Goldberg device to demonstrate knowledge of physics concepts and applications, and present the information in a video to the class.

13.4 Plan for Feedback

The Fourth Principle of Good Practice emphasizes prompt feedback to students. Students need to know how they are performing and what they can do to improve. In online courses, instructors use formative assessment information to communicate information that helps students reflect on their learning and set goals for future learning. Students can use feedback to monitor their progress toward learning goals, determine what their learning needs, and take more control of their learning (Bonnel, 2008).

 You must plan how and when you will give feedback to your students. Integrate feedback during the course planning and building stages. Bonnel developed several strategies to increase opportunities for providing feedback to students which are included below.

• Develop multiple sources of feedback for students (self-reflection, peer review, personalized and group responses).

• Develop introductory or orientation material with information about course feedback and student and faculty expectations and responsibilities.

• Include automated responses on computer-graded assignments.

• Develop intermittent deadlines for progress-monitoring of major projects to give students feedback as they work. Offer feedback to improve performance on the overall project submission.

Good feedback involves more than comments from the instructor; students value peer input as well as automated feedback and self-reflection (Bonnel, Ludwig and Smith, 2008). Automated feedback can be accomplished through the use of an online homework system, or by including feedback into quizzes and assignments built into the learning management system. Peer review can be implemented in several ways, depending on the type of assessment.

In Chapter 11, we discussed group collaboration and how students can review their peers using a rubric. If you require essays or other writing assignments in your courses, you can facilitate peer review by using discussion forums. Students can post a rough draft and other students can comment on what they like and what they think can be improved. Francis Pengitore suggests using the Track Changes function of Microsoft Word to suggest edits and comment on the reasoning behind the edits. The Review function simplifies the commenting and editing process, and allows color coding of comments. These functions can be used in a peer review process to allow students to ask questions and make suggestions on other students' papers (Pengitore, 2005). Google Docs has similar functionality, and can be utilized by multiple students at one time. Inserting comments directly into the paper can avoid confusion about what parts of the paper students are discussing. To encourage constructive feedback, instructors can provide a model of feedback expectations. If students simply say they like the paper, it doesn't help a student improve his or her writing.

The Fifth Principle of Good Practice emphasizes time on task. In a face-to-face course, you would notice if a student was not attending or was off task, and you could provide feedback to that student to encourage them to increase their time on task. In online classes, you can monitor student progress on assignments and provide feedback on those assignments, but you can also monitor how much time students are spending working in the learning management system. Reports can identify which students are not spending as much time in the course as others, and you can contact those students to encourage more participation.

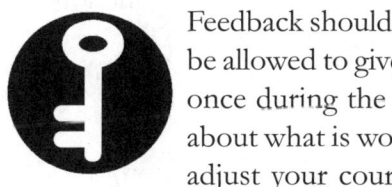 Feedback should not be in one direction. Students should be allowed to give feedback to instructors as well. At least once during the semester, seek feedback from students about what is working well for them and what is not, and adjust your course to better meet their needs as much as possible. In addition, colleges typically seek an end-of-semester evaluation survey from students. Analyze those results. You'll be able to determine which types of activities help students more than others and modify future courses to better accommodate for diverse talents and ways of learning, Seventh Principle of Good Practice (Chickering and Gamson, 1987). However, those end-of-course

evaluations do nothing to help students while they are taking the course. In an online course, it is important to actively seek feedback from your students sooner, and more often.

Make it clear in your syllabus and course orientation that students should contact you immediately if something does not work correctly or if they have any questions. Links will break from time to time as websites are updated. You may even find that you'll have an enterprising student who lets you know the link is broken, *and* sends you the updated link.

A quick survey of students as to what is working well for them and what is not lets you know in real time what you need to modify as you go through the semester. Remember that investing more time up front when planning allows you time during the semester to modify your course, as needed. Natalie Milman, of George Washington University, calls such requests for feedback during the semester the "Mid-Term Tune-Up." In her survey, Milman informs students that their responses are anonymous and voluntary and will not affect their grades (This is vital to receiving honest feedback). She then asks students what they feel most helps their learning in the course, and what changes could be made to improve their learning (Milman, 2014).

One semester, I had several athletes who asked during my own Mid-Term Tune-up survey to download lectures rather than streaming them online. The students wanted to use time on the bus to and from games to watch lecture recordings. I made that function available to them. Several free survey tools are available, and you can create the survey and email students a link and/or post a link in an announcement for students:

Google Forms – Create free forms with unlimited questions and distinctive design themes. Responses can be organized into Google Sheets or viewed within the Forms app itself

SurveyPlanet – With the free version, add unlimited questions and collect unlimited responses. In addition, surveyers can select themes for their surveys (SurveyPlanet).

ZOHO Survey – With the free version, add up to 15 questions and collect responses from up to 150 people.

SurveyMonkey – With the free version, you can add up to 10 questions and collect responses from up to 100 people.

I use Google Forms most often, though for a mid-semester student survey, any of the survey platforms above would work. Keep the survey fairly short so it won't take too much time. Create a separate survey for each class, so survey response limits are not an issue. If you have never used an online survey tool, you might want to try each of the tools above to determine which best suits your needs and those of your students.

When analyzing survey responses during the semester, there will be some aspects of your online science course you can change, some you cannot change, and some you may not want to change. For example, you may be able to offer some files in different formats, or make some items available for download so that students can access them when they do not have access to Internet. You may not be able to change how much material the course covers in a semester, and you may not want to change a group collaboration requirement. Even when I could not or would not change something during a class, I explained why, and students seemed to appreciate being heard, even if their recommendations were not adopted.

What is an Assessment Rubric?

Assessment rubrics can be used for any assessment task. They are most often designed as one-page grids that list a series of criteria and expectations for different levels of performance. They are filled out and returned with the student's assessment.

An assessment rubric serves several important functions:

- It makes the grading process explicit.

- It presents the criteria and the standards by which a student's work is being judged.

- It provides overall feedback in a clear, succinct way.

- It provides a focus for conversations about standards between teaching teams and between teachers and students.

CHAPTER 14
COMBATTING ACADEMIC DISHONESTY

14.1 Academic Dishonesty in Online Classes

Instructors of all course types encounter academic dishonesty in their classes. Is academic dishonesty more prevalent in online courses? Concrete answers are difficult to obtain due to conflicting and limited research. In a study from 2000, Kennedy et al. reported that most faculty and students felt it would be easier to cheat in online classes than in face-to-face classes, and suggested that academic dishonesty in online classes would increase along with the number of online classes (Kennedy, et al., 2000).

However, the results of multiple studies since 2000 refute the predictions of the Kennedy et al. study. Grijalva, Nowell, and Kerkvliet found that approximately 3 percent of students cheated in online classes, which is consistent with estimates of cheating in face-to-face courses (Grijalva, Nowell and Kerkvliet, 2006). A 2008 study indicated that 81 percent of students felt there was no more cheating in online classes than in face-to-face classes (Black, Greaser and Dawson).

In 2010, Watson and Sottile studied 635 undergraduate and graduate students and found that 32.1 percent of students reported cheating in a face-to-face class, versus 32.7 percent in an online class. Although the total percent is slightly higher for online classes, more students admitted cheating in online classes than in face-to-face courses, with one notable exception: cheating on tests and quizzes. More students in online classes reported obtaining test and quiz answers and instant messaging during a test or quiz (Watson and Sottile, 2010).

In 2012, a study by Miller and Young-Jones reported that 57.2 percent of students believed it is easier to cheat in online classes. Students enrolled in online and face-to-face courses reported more cheating in their online courses. However, students enrolled in only online courses reported lower rates of cheating, which seemed to be related to student age in the study. Students enrolled in only online courses in the study were significantly older than students enrolled in both online and face-to-face courses (Miller and Young-Jones, 2012).

Though disparity in reported amounts of cheating in online classes exists, no one disputes the fact that cheating exists in all types of courses. As time moves on, students develop new methods of cheating, and instructors must stay aware and work to prevent as much academic dishonesty as possible. As online instructors, we must design courses that limit the potential for academic dishonesty. To do that, we must know what types of cheating we are likely to encounter.

In a study of 514 introductory science students, 38.9 percent of students observed students copying homework done by another student (Nelson, Nelson and Tichenor, 2013). In online classes, this could include sharing files and copying answers from the Internet. In that same study, 30.9 percent of students reported discussing test and quizzes answers. Students could form a group and work together to answer test questions. In online classes, this could be done via Skype or Google Hangouts, or students could screenshot test questions and send it to others for help.

One potential reason for the increase shown in the Watson and Sottile study (2010) in cheating during online exams is that there are multiple methods. When students take an online exam that is not proctored, they can look up answers on one computer while completing the exam on another. In addition, students could open a test and print, screenshot, or take a picture of the questions. Then they could disconnect their Internet, causing an error, and screenshot the error as evidence. They submit the evidence to the instructor along with a request to have the exam reopened. While the students are waiting for the instructor to reopen the exam, they can research answers to the test questions (Moten, Fitterer and Brazier, 2013).

Moten, Fitterer, and Brazier describe multiple methods of academic dishonesty used by students, in addition to cheating on exams:

- Students can collude on assignments, allowing others to do work for them.

- Students can copy information from the Internet to answer essay questions.

- Students can purchase answers to test questions via the Internet.

- Students can search for answers to questions on the Internet (Moten, Fitterer and Brazier, 2013).

The prevalence of cheating in online courses may not necessarily be more than what occurs in face-to-face courses. In addition, the methods of cheating in online courses may not all be different, but new ideas seem to pop up constantly. For example, I was browsing Pinterest when I saw a post made by a student to help increase the word length of an essay without actually writing more. The student wrote words at the end of the paragraph and then set the font color to white, so no one could see them. The words in white still contribute to the total word count of the paper.

14.2 Paid Academic Dishonesty

There is one type of academic dishonesty that is relatively new, and that is paid academic dishonesty. Two colleagues at McLennan Community College (Alex Shui, Professor of Economics, and Brad Turner, Associate Professor of Environmental Science) recently presented a workshop at our college's spring Professional Development Day titled "Pay Us to Take Your Class – Soliciting Scholastic Services on Twitter," in which they described how they posed as undergraduate students on Twitter and asked for help in their classes. The responses were immediate, numerous, and disheartening. Multiple people and what appeared to be businesses specializing in writing papers and completing online course work offered to help the needy "students" for fairly low cost (Shui and Turner, 2017).

Since papers written by these businesses are original and written to the specifications of the assignment, plagiarism detection software won't show that the papers are not the student's original work. So, how do you combat this? Turner suggests making it too expensive for the students to keep purchasing papers by requiring frequent submissions of drafts that must meet certain specifications. Other options are to include a statement in the syllabus that you may question students about their written work, and students must sufficiently explain their thought process and what they mean in parts of the paper. If they can't, those students will receive a failing grade (Shui and Turner, 2017).

At Western Carolina University, two instructors created a fake online course, and hired several students to cheat. The objective was to determine if the instructors could detect the deception. One of the students hired a company via a website on the Internet to take the class for him. The company agreed to complete all course requirements and earn the student a grade of A, all for under $1,000 (Malesky, Baley and Crow, 2016).

One assignment posed a problem for the student and the company: a live presentation. The company agreed to provide a script and PowerPoint file, but refused to do the live presentation. The student utilized the materials provided to complete the presentation. Though the instructors were actively searching for signs of academic dishonestly in their course, they could not determine that the student had hired a company to complete the course. In the end, the company fulfilled its promise to earn the student a grade of A (Malesky, Baley and Crow, 2016).

Based on the company's response to the live presentation requirement, it appears that while they are willing to impersonate students online, they are not willing to impersonate a student in any kind of live (face-to-face) situation. Shui and Turner found something similar when they solicited companies to complete online classes. After receiving multiple responses from companies offering to complete the online classes, the companies backed off when told the course required proctored exams. Why? Perhaps the reason is that face-to-face situations like proctored exams make it simpler to determine if the student who is enrolled in the course is the person who is taking the exams. Another reason could be that it is more difficult to cheat during a proctored exam, so the person taking the exam would have to know the material well enough to complete the course successfully.

14.3 Plagiarism Detection Tools

While plagiarism software will not detect whether an original paper was written by someone other than the student, it can help to detect writing that is not original. Most colleges allow you access to plagiarism detection software, either directly through the learning management system (Blackboard SafeAssign) or an outside service like TurnItIn that integrates into the LMS. When setting up your dropbox for the assignment, you can select whether to check each paper using this software. I recommend using it as a learning tool, since all too often I have found that students do not understand what constitutes plagiarism. Some students think it's ok to copy text if you cite the source, while others think it's ok to have an entire paper made up of quotes from sources.

Plagiarism detection software compares each student submission against a bank of previously submitted papers, as well as other outside sources. The software then compares the text and highlights portions of the paper that correspond to portions of other papers and generates an originality report. The originality report shows the total percent of the student's paper that matches text found in other sources. For example, let's say that a student submits an assignment, and the originality report shows 25 percent similarity. At first, that sounds really bad, but you have to view the details of the report to know for certain. It could be 1 percent from 25 different sources that added up to 25 percent, or it could be 25 percent from one source. 1 percent from 25 different sources is likely due to common phrasing and works cited lists.

I view the originality report as another type of feedback for students that supports the Fourth Principle of Good Practice (Chickering and Gamson, 1987), so I allow students to view the originality report and rewrite their papers before the deadline if they find a problem. I usually tell them to look for entire sentences and large blocks of text that are highlighted on the report. Since the software picks up on common phrasing and sources, you'll need to alert students to what is important in the report. This gives those students who do not fully understand plagiarism a chance to view the report and learn from it.

14.4 Exam Proctoring Options

Can we eliminate all forms of academic dishonesty? It's not likely, but we can stay aware of trends and try to make it more difficult. Written assignments are not the only type of class assignment that students will attempt to cheat on. An estimated 50 percent of students attempt to cheat on online exams that have no proctoring process in place (UB Custom Publishing, 2017).

Obviously, the goal of proctoring exams is to try to prevent cheating during the exam, but it can also keep students from sharing information about the exam with other students who may not have taken the test yet. Because of this, you should require proctored exams in your courses, and it's easier than you might think.

Students who live close enough to campus can drive to the campus testing center and take the test there during the exam window. However, days and hours could be limited, and students who work might not be able to schedule a convenient time.

Students who cannot take their exams at the college testing center due to distance could use another campus or college testing center. They would have to give you the information with enough lead time to coordinate with that testing center. If work is the issue, or a student cannot make it to a testing center, there is another option: ProctorU.

ProctorU is an online proctoring company that students and colleges can use. Colleges can require that students use ProctorU, or make it optional. There are multiple ways of paying for exam proctoring as well. Colleges can contract with ProctorU and include the proctoring fees into the cost of the course. Alternatively, students can pay the proctoring fees separately (Institutions: ProctorU). Regardless, you should include a statement in your syllabus that all proctoring fees are the responsibility of the student, and explain the process.

I took an online graduate course through the University of Florida, and the proctoring fees were included in the tuition and fees I paid for the course. I set up proctoring appointments with ProctorU through the LMS, and only had to pay extra fees (approximately $5-$10) if I scheduled or changed an appointment within 72 hours of the exam window. Students paying directly for ProctorU exam proctoring will pay approximately $20-$40 per exam, depending on the length of the exam.

The proctoring experience was straightforward. I logged into the LMS at the scheduled time and clicked the link to begin the proctoring session. I was surprised by the verification questions, since they seemed like questions I have been asked in the past to verify my identity when I requested a credit report. I also had to show an ID and use the camera to show all parts of the room I was in. I interacted with the proctor, who walked me through the process, and the webcam on my laptop was used to view my activity during the exam.

Another online proctoring option is software that your college may have a license for already: Respondus. Respondus LockDown Browser integrates with your learning management system (Blackboard, Brightspace/D2L, Canvas, Moodle, Schoology, and Sakai) to restrict use of applications on a computer during a Respondus-enabled assignment. Students cannot copy, print, open other browser windows to search for answers on the Internet, or pull up information from files stored on the computer (Respondus - Assessment Tools for Learning Systems).

Respondus LockDown Browser cannot restrict the student from using another device, hard copies of notes, their textbook, or a friend, however. To prevent that, you'll need more than just the LockDown Browser; you'll need Respondus Monitor. Monitor uses webcam and video recording technology to proctor an exam without a person actually having to monitor the student. Students would take the exam online using the Respondus LockDown Browser, and Respondus Monitor records the student to ensure he/she is the person enrolled in the course, and that they do not access any inappropriate resources. Students can even be required to show ID to the camera before beginning the exam. Once the student submits the exam, a report is generated for the instructor, which contains pictures taken at random times, the student's grade, and time spent taking the exam. The full video is available if the instructor wishes to view it (Respondus Monitor).

Given the multiple options, finding a proctoring solution for your course should be relatively simple. I like to give students more than one option for proctoring, including the college testing center, ProctorU, and Respondus LockDown Browser / Monitor. I have allowed students to use other college testing centers in the past, but few used this option.

COPYRIGHT FAIR USE GUIDELINES FOR COLLEGE FACULTY

Courtesy of the Stanford Copyright and Fair Use Center, Stanford University Libraries, Stanford University, 2017 (http://fairuse.stanford.edu/).

What Types of Creative Work Does Copyright Protect?

Copyright protects works such as poetry, movies, CD-ROMs, video games, videos, plays, paintings, sheet music, recorded music performances, novels, software code, sculptures, photographs, choreography and architectural designs.

To qualify for copyright protection, a work must be "fixed in a tangible medium of expression." This means that the work must exist in some physical form for at least some period of time, no matter how brief. Virtually any form of expression will qualify as a tangible medium, including a computer's random access memory (RAM), the recording media that capture all radio and television broadcasts, and the scribbled notes on the back of an envelope that contain the basis for an impromptu speech.

In addition, the work must be original — that is, independently created by the author. It doesn't matter if an author's creation is similar to existing works, or even if it is arguably lacking in quality, ingenuity or aesthetic merit. So long as the author toils without copying from someone else, the results are protected by copyright.

Permission: What Is It and Why Do I Need It?

Obtaining copyright permission is the process of getting consent from a copyright owner to use the owner's creative material. Obtaining permission is often called "licensing"; when you have permission, you have a license to use the work. Permission is often (but not always) required because of intellectual property laws that protect creative works such as text, artwork, or music. If you use a copyrighted work without the appropriate permission, you may be violating—or "infringing"—the owner's rights to that work. Infringing someone else's copyright may subject you to legal action. As if going to court weren't bad enough, you could be forced to stop using the work or pay money damages to the copyright owner.

As noted above, permission is not always required. In some situations, you can reproduce a photograph, a song, or text without a license. Generally, this will be true if the work has fallen into the public domain, or if your use qualifies as what's called a "fair use." Both of these legal concepts involve quite specific rules. In most cases, however, permission is required, so it is important to never assume that it is okay to use a work without permission.

Many people operate illegally, either intentionally or through ignorance. They use other people's work and never seek consent. This may work well for those who fly under the radar—that is, if copyright owners never learn of the use, or don't care enough to take action.

Obtaining Clearance for Coursepacks

It is the instructor's obligation to obtain clearance for materials used in class. Instructors typically delegate this task to one of the following:

- Clearance services. These services are the easiest method of clearance and assembly.

- University bookstores or copy shops. University policies may require that the instructor delegate the task to the campus bookstore, copy shop, or to a special division of the university that specializes in clearances.

Using a Clearance Service

It can be time-consuming to seek and obtain permission for the 20, 30, or more articles you want to use in a coursepack. Fortunately, private clearance services will, for a fee, acquire permission and assemble coursepacks on your behalf. After the coursepacks are created and sold, the clearance service collects royalties and distributes the payments to the rights holders. Educational institutions may require that the instructor use a specific clearance service.

The largest copyright clearing service is the Copyright Clearance Center (www.copyright.com), which clears millions of works from thousands of publishers and authors.

In 2001, XanEdu (www.xanedu.com), acquired the coursepack service formerly known as Campus Custom Publishing. In addition to providing traditional coursepack assembly, XanEdu offers an electronic online service that provides supplemental college course materials directly to the instructor's desktop via the internet.

Educational Uses of Non-Coursepack Materials

Unlike academic coursepacks, other copyrighted materials can be used without permission in certain educational circumstances under copyright law or as a fair use. "Fair use" is the right to use portions of copyrighted materials without permission for purposes of education, commentary or parody.

The Code of Best Practices in Fair Use for Media Literacy Education

In 2008, the Center for Media and Social Impact, in connection with American University, unveiled a guide of fair use practices for instructors in K–12 education, in higher education, in nonprofit organizations that offer programs for children and youth, and in adult education. The guide identifies five principles that represent acceptable practices for the fair use of copyrighted materials. You can learn more at the center's website, (www.cmsimpact.org).

Guidelines Establish a Minimum, Not a Maximum

In a case alleging 75 instances of infringement in an educational setting, 70 instances were not infringing because of fair use and for other reasons. The infringements were alleged because of the posting of copyrighted books within a university's e-reserve system. The court viewed the Copyright Office's 1976 Guidelines for Educational Fair Use as a minimum, not a maximum standard. The court then proposed its own fair use standard—10% of a book with less than ten chapters, or of a book that is not divided into chapters, or no more than one chapter or its equivalent in a book of more than ten chapters.—*Cambridge University Press v. Georgia State University*, Case 1:08-cv-01425-OD (N.D. Ga., May 11, 2012).

What is the Difference Between the Guidelines and Fair Use Principles?

The educational guidelines are similar to a treaty that has been adopted by copyright owners and academics. Under this arrangement, copyright owners will permit uses that are outlined in the guidelines. In other fair use situations, the only way to prove that a use is permitted is to submit the matter to court or arbitration. In other words, in order to avoid lawsuits, the various parties have agreed on what is permissible for educational uses, codified in these guidelines.

What is an "Educational Use?"

The educational fair use guidelines apply to material used in educational institutions and for educational purposes. Examples of "educational institutions" include K-12 schools, colleges, and universities. Libraries, museums, hospitals, and other nonprofit institutions also are considered educational institutions under most educational fair use guidelines when they engage in nonprofit instructional, research, or scholarly activities for educational purposes.

Educational Purposes are:

- noncommercial instruction or curriculum-based teaching by educators to students at nonprofit educational institutions

- planned noncommercial study or investigation directed toward making a contribution to a field of knowledge, or

- presentation of research findings at noncommercial peer conferences, workshops, or seminars.

Rules for Reproducing Text Materials for Use in Class

The guidelines permit a teacher to make one copy of any of the following: a chapter from a book; an article from a periodical or newspaper; a short story, short essay, or short poem; a chart, graph, diagram, drawing, cartoon, or picture from a book, periodical, or newspaper.

Teachers may not photocopy workbooks, texts, standardized tests, or other materials that were created for educational use. The guidelines were not intended to allow teachers to usurp the profits of educational publishers. In other words, educational publishers do not consider it a fair use if the copying provides replacements or substitutes for the purchase of books, reprints, periodicals, tests, workbooks, anthologies, compilations, or collective works.

Rules for Reproducing Music

A music instructor can make copies of excerpts of sheet music or other printed works, provided that the excerpts do not constitute a "performable unit," such as a whole song, section, movement, or aria. In no case can more than 10% of the whole work be copied and the number of copies may not exceed one copy per pupil. Printed copies that have been purchased may be edited or simplified provided that the fundamental character of the work is not distorted or the lyrics altered.

A student may make a single recording of a performance of copyrighted music for evaluation or rehearsal purposes, and the educational institution or individual teacher may keep a copy. In addition, a single copy of a sound recording owned by an educational institution or an individual teacher (such as a tape, disc, or cassette) of copyrighted music may be made for the purpose of constructing aural exercises or examinations, and the educational institution or individual teacher can keep a copy.

Rules for Recording and Showing Television Programs

Nonprofit educational institutions can record television programs transmitted by network television and cable stations. The institution can keep the tape for 45 days, but can only use it for instructional purposes during the first ten of the 45 days. After the first ten days, the video recording can only be used for teacher evaluation purposes, to determine whether or not to include the broadcast program in the teaching curriculum. If the teacher wants to keep it within the curriculum, he or she must obtain permission from the copyright owner. The recording may be played once by each individual teacher in the course of related teaching activities in classrooms and similar places devoted to instruction (including formalized home instruction). The recorded program can be repeated once if necessary, although there are no standards for determining what is and is not necessary. After 45 days, the recording must be erased or destroyed.

A video recording of a broadcast can be made only at the request of and only used by individual teachers. A television show may not be regularly recorded in anticipation of requests—for example, a teacher cannot make a standing request to record each episode of a PBS series. Only enough copies may be reproduced from each recording to meet the needs of teachers, and the recordings may not be combined to create teaching compilations. All copies of a recording must include the copyright notice on the broadcast program as recorded and (as mentioned above) must be erased or destroyed after 45 days.

References

Abdelmalak, Mariam Mousa Matta. "Web 2.0 Technologies and Building Online Learning: Students' Perspectives." Online Learning, vol. 19, no.2, 01 Mar. 2015. EBSCOhost, ezproxy.mclennan.edu/login?url=http://search.ebscohost.com/login.aspx?direct=true&db=eric&AN=EJ1062942&site=eds-live.

"About: Google Forms." Google. https://www.google.com/forms/about/. Accessed 28 October 2017.

"About the Licenses." Creative Commons. www.creativecommons.org/licenses.

Allen, I. Elaine and Jeff Seaman. Changing Course: Ten Years of Tracking Online Education in the United States. Sloan Consortium, Babson Survey Research Group and Quahog Research Group, LLC., 01 Jan. 2013. http://files.eric.ed.gov/fulltext/ED541571.pdf??.

Allen, I. Elaine, et al. Online Report Card: Tracking Online Education in the United States. Babson Survey Research Group and Quahog Research Group, LLC., 01 Feb. 2016. EBSCOhost, ezproxy.mclennan.edu/login?url=http://search.ebscohost.com/login.aspx?direct=true&db=eric&AN=ED572777&site=eds-live.

Anderson, Merrilee. "Assessing Student Learning in the Introductory Microbiology Lab." ASM Education Blog. 24 April 2017. www.asm.org/index.php/education-blog/item/6383-assessing-student-learning-in-the-introductory-microbiology-lab. Accessed 10 October 2017.

Angelino, Lorraine M., Frankie Keels Williams and Deborah Natvig. "Strategies to Engage Online Students and Reduce Attrition Rates." The Journal of Educators Online, vol. 4, no. 2, 01 July 2007. EBSCOhost, ezproxy.mclennan.edu/login?url=http://search.ebscohost.com/login.aspx?direct=true&db=eric&AN=EJ907749&site=eds-live.

Atchley, Wayne, Gary Wingenbach and Cindy Akers. "Comparison of Course Completion and Student Performance through Online and Traditional Courses." The International Review of Research in Open and Distance Learning, vol. 14, no. 4, 2013, pp. 104-116. EBSCOhost, ezproxy.mclennan.edu/login?url=http://search.ebscohost.com/login.aspx?direct=true&db=ofm&AN=90653 412&site=eds-live.

Baker, D. L. "Advancing Best Practices for Asynchronous Online Discussion." Business Education Innovation Journal, vol. 5, no. 1, 2013, pp. 11-21. EBSCOhost, ezproxy.mclennan.edu/login?url=http://search.ebscohost.com/login.aspx?direct=true&db=bth&AN=89736811&site=eds-live.

Basu, Kaustuv. "Loss of Control." Inside Higher Ed. 14 March 2012. https://www.insidehighered.com/news/2012/03/14/former-asu-professors-threatens-litigation-over-online-course-ownership.

Battista, Ludmila and Verlinda Ruble. "Nine Strategies to Spark Adult Students' Intrinsic Motivation." Faculty Focus. 13 January 2014. Faculty Focus. www.facultyfocus.com/articles/teaching-and-learning/nine-strategies-to-spark-adult-students-intrinsic-motivation/.

Bernard, Robert M., et al. "How Does Distance Education Compare with Classroom Instruction? A Meta-Analysis of the Empirical Literature." Review of Educational Research, vol. 74, no. 3, 2004, pp. 412-413. EBSCOhost, ezproxy.mclennan.edu/login?url=http://search.ebscohost.com/login.aspx?direct=true&db=edsjsr&AN=edsjsr.3516028&site=eds-live.

BestColleges.com. Online Education Trends. Houston, Texas: BestColleges.com, 2016. http://www.bestcolleges.com/wp-content/uploads/2017-Online-Education-Trends-Report.pdf.

Black, Erik W., Joe Greaser and Kara Dawson. "Academic Dishonesty in Traditional and Online Classrooms: Does the "Media Equation" Hold True?" Journal of Asynchronous Learning Networks, vol. 12, no. 3-4, 2008, pp. 23-30. EBSCOhost, ezproxy.mclennan.edu/login?url=http://search.ebscohost.com/login.aspx?direct=true&db=eric&AN=EJ837484&site=eds-live.

Bonnel, Wanda. "Improving Feedback to Students in Online Courses." Nursing Education Perspectives, vol. 29, no. 5, 2008, pp. 290-294. EBSCOhost, ezproxy.mclennan.edu/login?url=http://search.ebscohost.com/login.aspx?direct=true&db=cmedm&AN=18834059&site=eds-live.

Bonnel, Wanda, Charlene Ludwig and Janice Smith. "Chapter 11. Providing Feedback in Online Courses: What Do Students Want? How Do We Do That?" Annual Review of Nursing Education, vol. 6, 2008, pp. 205-221. EBSCOhost, ezproxy.mclennan.edu/login?url=http://search.ebscohost.com/login.aspx?direct=true&db=c8h&AN=105888835&site=eds-live.

Bowman, Charles R., Ozcan Gulacar and Daniel B. King. "Predicting Student Success Via Online Homework Usage." Journal of Learning Design, vol. 7, no. 2, 2014, pp. 47-61. EBSCOhost, ezproxy.mclennan.edu/login?url=http://search.ebscohost.com/login.aspx?direct=true&db=eric&AN=EJ1040452&site=eds-live.

Brinson, Jim and Kasie Brinson. "Virtual and Remote Science Lab Effectiveness: What the Research Says." 30th Annual Conference on Distance Teaching and Learning Conference Proceedings 2014. Madison, WI: University of Wisconsin, 2014, pp. 322-326.

Brooks, D. Christopher. ECAR Study of Undergraduate Students and Information Technology, 2016. Research Report. Louisville, CO: EDUCAUSE, 2016. library.educause.edu/resources/2017/10/ecar-study-of-undergraduate-students-and-information-technology-2017.

Burgstahler, Sheryl. "ADA Compliance for Online Course Design." 30 January 2017. Educause Review. er.educause.edu/articles/2017/1/ada-compliance-for-online-course-design.

Burton, Rebecca S. "Readability, Logodiversity, and Effectiveness of College Science Textbooks." Bioscene, vol. 40, no. 1, 2014, pp. 3-10. EBSCOhost, ezproxy.mclennan.edu/login?url=http://search.ebscohost.com/login.aspx?direct=true&db=eric&AN=EJ1035554&site=eds-live.

Butler, Melanie B. and Ryan J. Zerr. "The Use of Online Homework Systems to Enhance Out-of-Class Engagement." International Journal for Technology in Mathematics Education, vol. 12, no. 2, 2005, pp. 51-58. EBSCOhost, ezproxy.mclennan.edu/login?url=http://search.ebscohost.com/login.aspx?direct=true&db=eric&AN=EJ874188&site=eds-live.

Butrymowicz, Sarah. Online Courses: Professors Peeved to Learn They Don't Own MOOCs. 3 March 2014. nation.time.com/2014/03/01/online-courses-moocs-ownership/print/.

Bybee, Rodger W. "Guest Editorial: The BSCS 5E Instructional Model: Personal Reflections and Contemporary Implications." Science and Children, 2014, pp. 10-13. static.nsta.org/files/sc1408_10.pdf.

Bybee, Rodger W., et al. The BSCS 5E Instructional Model: Origins and Effectiveness. Colorado Springs: BSCS, 2006. <bscs.org/sites/default/files/_media/about/downloads/BSCS_5E_Full_Report.pdf>.

Cain, Sean and Mike Laird. The Fundamental 5: The Formula for Quality Instruction. CreateSpace Independent Publishing Platform, 2011.

Carr, Sarah. "As Education Comes of Age, the Challenge Is Keeping the Students." Chronicle of Higher Education, 2000, pp. A39-A41. www.chronicle.com/article/As-Distance-Education-Comes-of/14334.

Carson-Newman University. "Copyright Guide for Online Course, E-Reserves, and Course Management Systems." Carson-Newman University Stephens-Burnett Memorial Library. library.cn.edu/CopyrightTips.pdf.

Cattaneo, Kelsey Hood. "Telling Active Learning Pedagogies Apart: from Theory to Practice." Journal of New Approaches in Educational Research, vol. 6, no. 2, 2017, pp. 144-152. EBSCOhost, ezproxy.mclennan.edu/login?url=http://search.ebscohost.com/login.aspx?direct=true&db=eric&AN=EJ1151062&site=eds-live.

Center for Educational Innovation. "Time and Cost Considerations in Developing an Online Course." 2017. Online Learning. cei.umn.edu/support-services/online-learning/time-and-cost-considerations-developing-online-course.

Chapman, Sandy and Patty Cantrell. "What is an Instructional Designer?" The Institute for Learning and Teaching. tilt.colostate. edu/teachingResources/tips/tip.cfm?tipid=70.

Chen, Xianglei. STEM Attrition: College Students' Paths Into and Out of STEM Fields. Institute of Education Sciences. Washington, DC: US Department of Education, 2013. nces.ed.gov/ pubs2014/2014001rev.pdf.

Chickering, Arthur W. and Zelda F. Gamson. "Seven Principles for Good Practice in Undergraduate Education." AAHE Bulletin, 1987, pp. 3-7. EBSCOhost, ezproxy.mclennan.edu/ login?url=http://search.ebscohost.com/login.aspx?direct=true &db=eric&AN=ED282491&site=eds-live.

Conaway, Wendy and Barbara Zorn-Arnold. "The Keys to Online Learning for Adults: The Six Principles of Andragogy." Distance Learning, vol. 12, no. 4, 2015, pp. 37-42. EBSCOhost, ezproxy. mclennan.edu/login?url=http://search.ebscohost.com/login.as px?direct=true&db=ofm&AN=114727542&site=eds-live.

Crews, Kenneth D. "Copyright and Distance Education: Making Sense of the TEACH Act." Change, vol. 6, 2003, p. 34.

Dale, Edgar. "A Truncated Section of the Cone of Experience." Theory into Practice, April 1970, pp. 96-100.

Dalman, Michael. "Re: Online Course Syllabus." 23 August 2017. Received by Frances Karels.

"Data Calculator." Verizon Wireless. 2017. www.verizonwireless.com/ data-calculator/.

de Lima, Mariana and Marta Zorrilla. "Social Networks and the Building of Learning Communities: An Experimental Study of a Social MOOC." International Review of Research in Open and Distributed Learning, vol. 18, no. 1, 2017, pp. 40-63. EBSCOhost, ezproxy.mclennan.edu/login?url=http://search.ebscohost. com/login.aspx?direct=true&db=eric&AN=EJ1136087&site =eds-live.

deNoyelles, Aimee, John Raible and Ryan Seilhamer. "Exploring Students' E-Textbook Practices in Higher Education." Educause

Review. 6 July 2016. er.educause.edu/articles/2015/7/exploring-students-etextbook-practices-in-higher-education.

"Distance Education Policies, Procedures, and Forms." Texas Higher Education Coordinating Board. thecb.state.tx.us/index.cfm?objectid=A5A152AC-D29D-334F-872625E9E77B3B37.

Dykes, Jeff. "Task Books as an Assessment Tool for Demonstrating Basic Lab Skills in a Microbiology Course." Journal of Microbiology and Biology Education, vol. 13, no. 1, 2012, pp. 57-58. EBSCOhost, doi:10.1128/jmbe.v13i1.350.

Edwards, Renee, Audrey Mattoon and Heather McKay. Findings and Recommendations North American Network of Science Labs Online (NANSLO). School of Management and Labor Relations. Piscataway, NJ: Rutgers University, 2015. smlr.rutgers.edu/sites/default/files/documents/NANSLO%20Report%20Final%207-1-15.pdf.

Egbert, Joy and Mary F. Roe. "The Power of Why: Connecting Curriculum to Students' Lives." Childhood Education, vol. 90, no. 4, 2014, pp. 251-258. EBSCOhost, doi:10.1080/00094056.2014.933665.

Eisenkraft, Arthur. "Closing the Gap: Laboratory Experiences, and Not Just Textbooks, Are the Best Way to Provide Equal Learning Opportunities for All." Science Teacher, vol. 80, no. 4, 2013, pp. 42-45. EBSCOhost, ezproxy.mclennan.edu/login?url=http://search.ebscohost.com/login.aspx?direct=true&db=edsjsr&AN=edsjsr.43557182&site=eds-live.

Elvers, G. C., D. J. Polzella and K. Graetz. "Procrastination in Online Courses: Performance and Attitudinal Differences." Teaching of Psychology, vol. 30, no. 2, Spring 2003, pp. 159-162. EBSCOhost, ezproxy.mclennan.edu/login?url=http://search.ebscohost.com/login.aspx?direct=true&db=a9h&AN=9552194&site=eds-live.

Epper, Rhonda M. "Colorado Study Finds "No Significant Difference" in Online Science Courses." WCET Frontiers. 10 October 2012. wcetfrontiers.org/2012/10/18/co_nsd/.

Freeman, Lee A. "Instructor Time Requirements to Develop and Teach Online Courses." Online Journal of Distance Learning Administration, vol. 18, no. 1, Spring 2015. www.westga.edu/~distance/ojdla/spring181/freeman181.html.

Freeman, Scott, et al. "Prescribed Active Learning Increases Performance in Introductory Biology." Cell Biology Education Life Sciences Education, vol. 6, no. 2, 2007, pp. 132-139. EBSCOhost, ezproxy.mclennan.edu/login?url=http://search.ebscohost.com/login.aspx?direct=true&db=cmedm&AN=17548875&site=eds-live.

French, Michelle, et al. "Textbook Use in the Sciences and Its Relation to Course Performance." College Teaching, vol. 63, no. 4, 2015, pp. 171-177. EBSCOhost, ezproxy.mclennan.edu/login?url=http://search.ebscohost.com/login.aspx?direct=true&db=f5h&AN=110319066&site=eds-live.

Getzlaf, Beverley; Perry, Beth; Toffner, Greg; Lamarche, Kimberley; Edwards, Margaret. "Effective Instructor Feedback: Perceptions of Online Graduate Students." Journal of Educators Online , vol. 6 no. 2, 2009.

"Google Voice Features." Google. www.google.com/googlevoice/about.html#tab=oneNumber.

Grijalva, Therese C., Clifford Nowell and Joe Kerkvliet. "Academic Honesty and Online Courses." College Student Journal, vol. 40, no. 1, 2006, pp. 180-185. EBSCOhost, ezproxy.mclennan.edu/login?url=http://search.ebscohost.com/login.aspx?direct=true&db=eric&AN=EJ765312&site=eds-live.

Grinberg, Emanuella, Jamie Gumbrecht and Thom Patterson. "5 Ways Community Colleges Are Fixing Higher Education." CNN, 20 November 2014. www.cnn.com/2014/11/20/living/ivory-tower-community-colleges/index.html. Accessed 18 November 2017.

Guidera, Stan G. "Perceptions of the Effectiveness of Online Instruction in Terms of the Seven Principles of Effective Undergraduate Education." Journal of Educational Technology Systems, vol. 32, no. 2/3, 2003-2004, pp. 139-178. EBSCOhost, ezproxy.mclennan.edu/login?url=http://search.ebscohost.com/login.aspx?direct=true&db=cph&AN=13839178&site=eds-live.

Harvard University. "Active Learning." Derek Bok Center for Teaching and Learning. bokcenter.harvard.edu/active-learning. 21 November 2017.

Hathaway, Karen L. "An Application of the Seven Principles of Good Practice to Online Courses." Research in Higher Education Journal, vol. 22, 01 Feb. 2014. EBSCOhost, ezproxy.mclennan.edu/login?url=http://search.ebscohost.com/login.aspx?direct=true&db=eric&AN=EJ1064101&site=eds-live.

Hensiek, Sarah, et al. "Digital Badges in Science: A Novel Approach to the Assessment of Student Learning." Journal of College Science Teaching, vol. 46, no. 3, 2017, pp. 28-33. EBSCOhost, ezproxy.mclennan.edu/login?url=http://search.ebscohost.com/login.aspx?direct=true&db=ofm&AN=120346710&site=eds-live.

Hess, Frederick. "Old School: College's Most Important Trend is the Rise of the Adult Student." The Atlantic, 28 September 2011. www.theatlantic.com/business/archive/2011/09/old-school-colleges-most-important-trend-is-the-rise-of-the-adult-student/245823/.

Hilton, III, John. "Open Educational Resources and College Textbook Choices: a Review of Research on Efficacy and Perceptions." Education Technology Research Development, vol. 64, no. 4, 2016, pp. 573-590. EBSCOhost, ezproxy.mclennan.edu/login?url=http://search.ebscohost.com/login.aspx?direct=true&db=eric&AN=EJ1108018&site=eds-live.

Hiltz, Starr Roxanne. "Impacts of College-Level Courses via Asynchronous Learning Networks: Some Preliminary Results." Journal of Asynchronous Learning Networks, vol. 1, no. 2, 1997, pp. 1-19. onlinelearningconsortium.org/sites/default/files/v1n2_hiltz_1.pdf.

Hunter, Bill and Roger Austin. "Building Community Through Online Learning in Colleges." College Quarterly, vol. 18, no. 1, 2015. EBSCOhost, ezproxy.mclennan.edu/login?url=http://search.ebscohost.com/login.aspx?direct=true&db=eric&AN=EJ1070029&site=eds-live.

Ingeno, L. "Faculty Responsible for Making Online Materials Accessible for Disabled Students." Inside Higher Ed. 24 June 2013. insidehighered.com/news/2013/06/24/faculty-responsible-for-making-online-materials-accessible-to-disabled-students.

"Institutions: ProctorU." ProctorU. https://www.proctoru.com/institutions/.

"Internet Data Calculator." AT&T. www.att.com/esupport/data-calculator/index.jsp.

John Wiley & Sons, Inc. "Unlikely Partners - Wiley and Open-Stax College - Create Innovative Product for College Biology [Press Release}." 2013. EBSCOhost, ezproxy.mclennan.edu/login?url=http://search.ebscohost.com/login.aspx?direct=true&db=bwh&AN=bizwire.c47455887&site=eds-live.

Johnson, Heather A. and Laura C. Barrett. "Your Teaching Strategy Matters: How Engagement Impacts Application in Health Information Literacy Instruction." Journal of the Medical Library Association, vol. 105, no. 1, 2017, pp. 44-48. EBSCOhost, doi:10.5195/jmla.2017.8.

Kennedy, Kristen, et al. "Academic Dishonesty and Distance Learning: Student and Faculty Views." The College Student Journal, vol. 34, no. 2, 2000, pp. 309-314. EBSCOhost, ezproxy.mclennan.edu/login?url=http://search.ebscohost.com/login.aspx?direct=true&db=a9h&AN=3452564&site=eds-live.

Kinney, Beth. Open at UD: Virtual Microscope. 30 Jan. 2014. sites.udel.edu/open/2014/01/30/virtual-microscope/.

Knowles, Malcolm S., Elwood F. III Holton and Richard A. Swanson. The Adult Learner [Electronic Resource]: The Definitive Classic in Adult Education and Human Resource Development. Amsterdam, Boston: Elsevier, 2005. EBSCOhost, ezproxy.mclennan.edu/login?url=http://search.ebscohost.com/login.aspx?direct=true&db=cat03346a&AN=mcl.60660590&site=eds-live.

Kolesnikova, Natalia A. "The Changing Role of Community Colleges." Bridges, Fall 2009. www.stlouisfed.org/publications/bridges/fall-2009/the-changing-role-of-community-colleges.

Lalley, James P. and Robert H. Miller. "The Learning Pyramid: Does It Point Teachers in the Right Direction." Education, vol. 128, no. 1, 2007, pp. 64-79. EBSCOhost, ezproxy.mclennan.edu/login?url=http://search.ebscohost.com/login.aspx?direct=true&db=a9h&AN=27238989&site=eds-live.

Laxman, Kumar and Yap Kueh Chin. "Impact of Simulations on the Mental Models of Students in the Online Learning of Science Concepts." Journal of School Educational Technology, vol. 7, no. 2, 2011, pp. 1-12. EBSCOhost, ezproxy.mclennan.edu/login?url=http://search.ebscohost.com/login.aspx?direct=true&db=eric&AN=EJ1102747&site=eds-live.

Legislative Budget Board Staff. "Overview of Funding Formulas for Institutions of Higher Education." May 2016. Legislative Budget Board. www.lbb.state.tx.us/Documents/Publications/Presentation/1982_Formula_Funding_Overview_Presentation.pdf.

Leonard, William H. "How Do College Students Best Learn Science?" Journal of College Science Teaching, vol. 29, no. 6, 2000, pp. 385-388. EBSCOhost, ezproxy.mclennan.edu/login?url=http://search.ebscohost.com/login.aspx?direct=true&db=eric&AN=EJ610507&site=eds-live.

Levine, Judith R. "The Effect of Different Attendance Policies on Student Attendance and Achievement." Annual Meeting of the Eastern Psychological Association. Boston, 3-5 April 1992. eric.ed.gov/?id=ED348762.

Lipson, Steven M. and Marina Gair. "The Recording of Student Performance in the Microbiology Laboratory as a Training, Tutorial, and Motivational Tool." Journal of Microbiology and Biology Education, vol. 12, no. 1, 2011, pp. 48-50. EBSCOhost, doi:10.1128/jmbe.v12i1.248.

LoPresto, Michael C. and Timothy F. Slater. "A New Comparison Of Active Learning Strategies To Traditional Lectures For Teaching College Astronomy." Journal of Astronomy & Earth Science Education, vol. 3, no. 1, 2016, pp. 59-76. EBSCOhost, ezproxy.mclennan.edu/login?url=http://search.ebscohost.com/login.aspx?direct=true&db=eric&AN=EJ1103065&site=eds-live.

Love, Tyler S. "Addressing Safety and Liability in STEM Education: A Review of Important Legal Issues and Case Law." The Journal of Technology Studies, vol. 39, no. 1, 2013, pp. 28-41. EBSCOhost, ezproxy.mclennan.edu/login?url=http://search.ebscohost.com/login.aspx?direct=true&db=a9h&AN=92527288&site=eds-live.

Luft, Julie. "Rubrics: Design and Use in Science Teacher Education." Annual Meeting of the Association for the Education of Teachers in Science. Minneapolis, 1998. EBSCOhost, ezproxy.mclennan.edu/login?url=http://search.ebscohost.com/login.aspx?direct=true&db=eric&AN=ED417145&site=eds-live.

Lyubartseva, Ganna and Uma Prasad Mallik. "Attendance and Student Performance in Undergraduate Chemistry Courses." Education, vol. 133, no. 1, 2012, pp. 31-34. EBSCOhost, ezproxy.mclennan.edu/login?url=http://search.ebscohost.com/login.aspx?direct=true&db=f5h&AN=79776628&site=eds-live.

Malesky, L. Alvin, Jr., John Baley and Robert Crow. "Academic Dishonesty: Assessing the Threat of Cheating Companies to Online Education." College Teaching, vol. 64, no. 4, 2016, pp. 178-183. EBSCOhost, ezproxy.mclennan.edu/login?url=http://search.ebscohost.com/login.aspx?direct=true&db=eric&AN=EJ1114477&site=eds-live.

Marorell, Ingrid and McIntire Theresa. "Online Homework and Student Achievement in a Large Enrollment Introductory Science Course." Journal of College Science Teaching, vol. 40, no. 6, 2011, pp. 70-79.

Matejka, Ken and Lance B. Kurke. "Designing a Great Syllabus." College Teaching, vol. 42, no. 3, 1994, pp. 115-117. EBSCOhost, ezproxy.mclennan.edu/login?url=http://search.ebscohost.com/login.aspx?direct=true&db=a9h&AN=9410194934&site=eds-live.

McGowan, Matthew K. and Paul R. Stephens. "College Textbook Acquisition: An Exploratory Study." Journal of Learning in Higher Education, vol. 11, no. 1, 2015, pp. 85-90. EBSCOhost, ezproxy.mclennan.edu/login?url=http://search.ebscohost.com/login.aspx?direct=true&db=eric&AN=EJ1141768&site=eds-live.

McLaughlin, Kevin and Henry Mandin. "A Schematic Approach to Diagnosing and Resolving Lecturalgia." Medical Education, vol. 35, no. 12, 2001, pp. 1135-1142. EBSCOhost, ezproxy.mclennan. edu/login?url=http://search.ebscohost.com/login.aspx?direct= true&db=cmedm&AN=11895238&site=eds-live.

Miller, Arden and Adena D. Young-Jones. "Academic Integrity: Online Classes Compared to Face-to-Face Classes." Journal of Instructional Psychology, vol. 39, no. 3/4, 2012, pp. 138-145. EBSCOhost, ezproxy.mclennan.edu/login?url=http://search. ebscohost.com/login.aspx?direct=true&db=a9h&AN=905393 00&site=eds-live.

Miller, Jon R., Andrew W. Nutting and Lori Baker-Eveleth. "The Determinants of Electronic Textbook Use Among College Students." American Economist, vol. 58, no. 1, 2013, pp. 41-50. EBSCOhost, ezproxy.mclennan.edu/login?url=http://search. ebscohost.com/login.aspx?direct=true&db=edsjsr&AN=edsjs r.43664819&site=eds-live.

Miller, Kenneth W. "Teaching Science Methods Online: Myths about Inquiry-based Online Learning." Science Educator, vol. 17, no. 2, 2008, pp. 80-86. EBSCOhost, ezproxy.mclennan.edu/ login?url=http://search.ebscohost.com/login.aspx?direct=true &db=eric&AN=EJ886175&site=eds-live.

Miller, Sandra and Gayle Stein. "Finding Our Voice: Instructional Designers in Higher Education." Educause Review, 8 February 2016. er.educause.edu/articles/2016/2/finding-our-voice-instructional-designers-in-higher-education.

Milman, Natalie B. "The Mid-Term Tune-Up: Getting Student Feedback Before It Is Too Late." Distance Learning, vol. 11, no. 4, 2014, pp. 51-53. EBSCOhost, ezproxy.mclennan.edu/ login?url=http://search.ebscohost.com/login.aspx?direct=true &db=ofm&AN=100558708&site=eds-live.

Mitchell, Travis. "10 Reasons to Attend a Community College." US News & World Report, 10 June 2015. www.usnews.com/education/community-colleges/slideshows/10-reasons-to-attend-a-community-college?slide=2.

Mo, Songtao. "The Clock is Ticking - An Analysis of Time Spent on Online Assignments." Academy of Educational Leadership Journal, vol. 19, no. 2, 2015, pp. 129-134. EBSCOhost, ezproxy. mclennan.edu/login?url=http://search.ebscohost.com/login.as px?direct=true&db=ofm&AN=111492324&site=eds-live.

Moltz, David. "Home Dissection Kits and More." Inside Higher Ed. 5 June 2009. www.insidehighered.com/news/2009/06/05/scien ce?width=775&height=500&iframe=true.

Moore, Randy. "Attendance and Performance: How Important Is It for Students to Attend Class?" Journal of College Science Teaching, vol. 32, no. 6, 2003, pp. 367-371. EBSCOhost, ezproxy.mclennan. edu/login?url=http://search.ebscohost.com/login.aspx?direct= true&db=edsjsr&AN=edsjsr.42991561&site=eds-live.

Morgan, Kari, et al. "Faculty Perceptions of Online Group Work." The Quarterly Review of Distance Education, vol. 15, no. 4, 2014, pp. 37-41. EBSCOhost, ezproxy.mclennan.edu/login?url=http:// search.ebscohost.com/login.aspx?direct=true&db=a9h&AN=1 01774143&site=eds-live.

Moten, James, Jr., Alex Fitterer and Elise Brazier. "Examining Online College Cyber Cheating Methods and Prevention Methods." Electronic Journal of E-Learning, vol. 11, no. 2, 2013, pp. 139-146. EBSCOhost, ezproxy.mclennan.edu/login?url=http://search. ebscohost.com/login.aspx?direct=true&db=eric&AN=EJ1012 879&site=eds-live.

Myers, Sandra. "Formative and Summative Assessments." Research Starters: Education (Online Edition) (2015).

National Academy of Sciences. Improving Adult Literacy Instruction: Supporting Learning and Motivation. Washington, DC: The National Academy Press, 2012. www.nap.edu/catalog/13469/ improving-adult-literacy-instruction-supporting-learning-and-motivation.

National Disability Authority. "Definition and Overview." Centre for Excellence in Universal Design. universaldesign.ie/what-is-universal-design/definition-and-overview/definition-and-overview. html. Accessed 22 November 2017.

Nehme, Zeina. "The Social Arena of the Online Synchronous Environment." Turkish Online Journal of Distance Education, vol. 9, no. 2, 2008, pp. 238-249. EBSCOhost, ezproxy.mclennan.edu/login?url=http://search.ebscohost.com/login.aspx?direct=true&db=eric&AN=ED501111&site=eds-live.

Nelson, Lynda P., Rodney K. Nelson and Linda Tichenor. "Understanding Today's Students: Entry-Level Science Student Involvement in Academic Dishonesty." Journal of College Science Teaching, vol. 42, no. 3, 2013, pp. 52-57. EBSCOhost, ezproxy.mclennan.edu/login?url=http://search.ebscohost.com/login.aspx?direct=true&db=edsjsr&AN=edsjsr.43631795&site=eds-live.

Nigro, Kirk A. "Science Teachers and Liability." Annual Meeting of the National Science Teachers Association. Portland, ME: National Science Teachers Association, 01 Oct. 1988. EBSCOhost, ezproxy.mclennan.edu/login?url=http://search.ebscohost.com/login.aspx?direct=true&db=eric&AN=ED299708&site=eds-live.

"OER Commons and Open Education." OER Commons. www.oercommons.org/about.

Office of Learning Technologies. Models of Community Learning Networks in Canada. Ottawa, Ontario, Canada: Office of Learning Technologies by New Economy Development Group Inc., 1998. files.eric.ed.gov/fulltext/ED431896.pdf.

"Online Learning Readiness Questionnaire." The University of North Carolina at Chapel Hill. www.unc.edu/tlim/ser/. Accessed 25 November 2017.

"Open Textbook 101." BCcampus Open Education. open.bccampus.ca/open-textbook-101/.

"Open Textbooks."Open Textbook Library. open.umn.edu/open-textbooks/.

Ouska, Julie. "Online Lab Kit Contract." 10 August 2016. Colorado Community College System. www.cccs.edu/Docs/SBCCOE/Agenda/2016/08Aug/2_WS_IC_CA_IVB_CCCOnlineLabKitContract.pdf.

Pengitore, Francis. "Effective Strategy for Providing Prompt Feedback on Writing Assignments When Teaching Courses Online." Online Classroom, Aug. 2005, p. 5. EBSCOhost, ezproxy.mclennan.edu/login?url=http://search.ebscohost.com/login.aspx?direct=true&db=a9h&AN=17749785&site=eds-live.

Perdian, David C. "Early Identification of Student Performance and Effort Using An Online Homework System: A Pilot Study." Journal of Science Education and Technology, vol. 22, no. 5, 2013, pp. 697-701. EBSCOhost, doi:10.1007/s10956-012-9423-7.

Pitt, Rebecca. "Mainstreaming Open Textbooks: Educator Prospectives on the Impact of OpenStax College Open Textbooks." International Review of Research in Open and Distributed Learning, vol. 16, no. 4, 2015, pp. 133-155. EBSCOhost, ezproxy.mclennan.edu/login?url=http://search.ebscohost.com/login.aspx?direct=true&db=eric&AN=EJ1082205&site=eds-live.

"Plans and Pricing." SurveyMonkey. www.surveymonkey.com/pricing/?ut_source=header. Accessed 28 October 2017.

Podolefsky, Noah and Noah Finkelstein. "The Perceived Value of College Physics Textbooks: Students and Instructors May Not See Eye to Eye." The Physics Teacher, vol. 44, no. 6, 2006, pp. 338-342. www.colorado.edu/physics/EducationIssues/textbooks/Podolefsky_Textbooks.pdf.

"Policies and Procedures: Class Attendance." McLennan Community College. 11 July 2016. www.mclennan.edu/employees/policy-manual/docs/B-II.pdf>. Accessed 20 October 2017.

Popken, Ben. "College Textbook Prices Have Risen 1041 Percent Since 1977." NBC News. www.nbcnews.com/feature/freshman-year/college-textbook-prices-have-risen-812-percent-1978-n399926. Accessed 12 November 2017.

Poulin, Russ. " Highlights of Distance Education Enrollment Trends from IPEDS Fall 2014." WCET Frontiers, 2014. wcetfrontiers.org/2015/12/21/ipeds-fall-2014-de-highlights/.

"Pricing." ZOHO Survey. www.zoho.com/survey/pricing.html. Accessed 28 October 2017.

Quality Matters. Course Design Reviews. 2017. www.qualitymatters. org/reviews-certifications/course-design-reviews.

"Quick Guide: College Costs." The College Board. bigfuture.collegeboard.org/pay-for-college/college-costs/quick-guide-college-costs. Accessed 13 November 2017.

Radford, Alexandria Walton, Melissa Cominole and Paul Skomsvold. "Demographic and Enrollment Characteristics of Nontraditional Undergraduates: 2011-12." National Center for Education Statistics. 9 September 2015. nces.ed.gov/pubs2015/2015025.pdf.

Ramesh D., Ingrid Marorell and Theresa M. McIntire. "Online Homework and Student Achievement in a Large Introductory Science Course." Journal of College Science Teaching, vol. 40, no.6, 2011, pp. 70-79. EBSCOhost, ezproxy.mclennan.edu/login?url=http:// search.ebscohost.com/login.aspx?direct=true&db=edsjsr&AN= edsjsr.42992900&site=eds-live.

Respondus - Assessment Tools for Learning Systems. www.respondus. com/lockdown-browser/index/shtml.

Respondus Monitor. www.respondus.com/products/monitor/index. shtml.

Richie, Sarah D. and David S. Hargrove. "An Analysis of the Effectiveness of Telephone Intervention in Reducing Absences and Improving Grades of College Freshmen." Journal of College Student Retention: Research, Theory & Practice, 2004, pp. 395-412. citeseerx.ist.psu.edu/viewdoc/download?doi=10.1.1.867.3 898&rep=rep1&type=pdf.

Risko, Evan F., et al. "Everyday Attention: Variation in Mind Wandering and Memory in a Lecture." Applied Cognitive Psychology, vol. 26, no. 2, 2012, pp. 234-242. EBSCOhost, doi:10.1002/acp.1814.

Ryan, Richard M. and Edward L. Deci. "Intrinsic and Extrinsic Motivations: Classic Definitions and New Directions." Contemporary Educational Psychology, vol. 25, 2000, pp. 54-67. www.sciencedirect.com/science/article/pii/S0361476X99910202.

Sahin, Sami. "Computer Simulations in Science Education: Implications for Distance Education." Turkish Online Journal of Distance Education, vol. 7, no. 4, 2006, pp. 1-13. EBSCOhost, ezproxy.mclennan.edu/login?url=http://search.ebscohost. com/login.aspx?direct=true&db=eric&AN=ED494379&site =eds-live.

Schwab, Joe. "Growing STEM Students: How Late Nite Labs' Online Platform Is Spreading Science And Saving Schools' Resources." J. Educational Technology Systems, vol. 41, no. 4, 2012-2013, pp. 333-345. EBSCOhost, doi:10.2190/ET.41.4.d.

Scott, James, Karen Swan and Cassandra Daston. "Retention, Progression and the Taking of Online Courses." Online Learning, vol. 20, no. 2, 2016, pp. 75-96. EBSCOhost, ezproxy.mclennan. edu/login?url=http://search.ebscohost.com/login.aspx?direct= true&db=eric&AN=EJ1105922&site=eds-live.

Senack, Ethan and Robert Donoghue. "Covering the Cost: Why We Can No Longer Afford to Ignore High Textbook Prices." The Student PIRGs. February 2016. studentpirgs.org/sites/student/ files/reports/National%20-%20COVERING%20THE%20 COST.pdf.

Shui, A and B. Turner. "Pay Us to Take Your Class - Soliciting Academic Services on Twitter." McLennan Community College Professional Development Day. Waco, TX, 24 March 2017.

Siegel, Jim. "ECOT Not Alone in Online Charter Schools' Attendance Struggles." Columbus Dispatch, 11 September 2016. www.dispatch.com/content/stories/local/2016/09/11/ecot-not-alone-in-attendance-struggles.html.

Slattery, Jeanne M. and Janet F. Carlson. "Preparing an Effective Syllabus." College Teaching, vol. 53, no. 4, 2005, pp. 159-164. EBSCOhost, ezproxy.mclennan.edu/login?url=http://search. ebscohost.com/login.aspx?direct=true&db=a9h&AN=187413 83&site=eds-live.

Soto, Julio G. and Anand Sulekha. "Factors Influencing Performance of Students Enrolled in a Lower Division Cell Biology Core Course." Journal of the Scholarship of Teaching and Learning, vol. 9, no. 1, 2009, pp. 64-80. EBSCOhost, ezproxy.mclennan. edu/login?url=http://search.ebscohost.com/login.aspx?direct= true&db=eric&AN=EJ854879&site=eds-live.

Strandberg, Alicia Granziosi and Kathleen Campbell. "Online Teaching Best Practices to Better Engage Students with Quantitative Material." Journal of Instructional Pedagogies, vol. 15, 01 Oct. 2014. EBSCOhost, ezproxy.mclennan.edu/login?url=http://search.ebscohost.com/login.aspx?direct=true&db=eric&AN=EJ1106761&site=eds-live.

Sull, Errol Craig. "The (Almost) Complete Guide to Effectively Managing Threaded Discussions." Distance Learning, vol. 11, no. 3, 2014, pp. 11-16. EBSCOhost, ezproxy.mclennan.edu/login?url=http://search.ebscohost.com/login.aspx?direct=true&db=ofm&AN=99016908&site=eds-live.

Sundaram, Premalata and Ross Roberts. "Check My Work! Instantaneous Feedback and Student Performance in an Introductory Financial Accounting Course." Proceedings of the Academy of Accounting & Financial Studies, vol. 20, no. 1, 2015, p. 34. EBSCOhost, ezproxy.mclennan.edu/login?url=http://search.ebscohost.com/login.aspx?direct=true&db=bth&AN=112640130&site=eds-live.

SurveyPlanet. surveyplanet.com/. Accessed 28 October 2017.

Technavio. Virtual and Remote Laboratories Market in the US 2016-2020. London: Technavio, 2016. new.technavio.com/report/usa-education-technology-virtual-and-remote-laboratories-market.

Ter-Stephanian, Anahit. "Online or Face to Face?: Instructional Strategies for Improving Learning Outcomes in e-Learning." The International Journal of Technology, Knowledge, and Society, vol. 8, no. 2, 2012, pp. 41-50. EBSCOhost, ezproxy.mclennan.edu/login?url=http://search.ebscohost.com/login.aspx?direct=true&db=a9h&AN=91544552&site=eds-live.

"Texas Core Curriculum." Texas Higher Education Coordinating Board. www.thecb.state.tx.us/apps/tcc. Accessed 11 November 2017.

"The Keys to Online Learning for Adults: The Six Principles of Andragogy, Part II." Distance Learning, vol. 13, no. 1, 2016, pp. 37-42. EBSCOhost, ezproxy.mclennan.edu/login?url=http://search.ebscohost.com/login.aspx?direct=true&db=ofm&AN=116352377&site=eds-live.

"The Three Principles of UDL." National Center on Universal Design for Learning. 18 September 2014. www.udlcenter.org/aboutudl/whatisudl/3principles. Accessed 22 November 2017.

Thompson, Ling and Heng-Yu Ku. "A Case Study of Online Collaborative Learning." The Quarterly Review of Distance Education, vol. 7, no. 4, 2006, pp. 361-375. EBSCOhost, ezproxy.mclennan.edu/login?url=http://search.ebscohost.com/login.aspx?direct=true&db=a9h&AN=23965560&site=eds-live.

Tu, Chih-Hsiung and Michael Corry. "Research in Online Learning Community." Journal of Instructional Science and Technology, vol. 5, no. 1, 2002. ascilite.org/archived-journals/e-jist/docs/Vol5_No1/chtu.html.

University of Minnesota Center for Educational Innovation. "Active Learning Classrooms | Center For Educational Innovation," 2017. https://cei.umn.edu/support-services/tutorials/active-learning-classrooms.

U.S. Copyright Office. Reproduction of Copyrighted Works by Educators and Librarians. Washington, D.C.: Library of Congress, 2014. www.copyright.gov/circs/circ21.pdf.

"U.S. Home Broadband and Wi-Fi Usage Forecast, 2015-2020: Increasing Usage in the Home." iGR. May 2016. igr-inc.com/advisory-subscription-services/wireless-mobile-landscape/us_home_broadband_wifi_forecast_2020.asp.

UB Custom Publishing. "An Insider's View of Online Proctoring." University Business Magazine, 23 February 2017. www.universitybusiness.com/article/insider-s-view-online-proctoring.

Ural, Evrim. "The Effect of Guided-Inquiry Laboratory Experiments on Science Education Students' Chemistry Laboratory Attitudes, Anxiety, and Achievement." Journal of Education and Training Studies, vol. 4, no. 4, 2016, pp. 217-227. EBSCOhost, ezproxy.mclennan.edu/login?url=http://search.ebscohost.com/login.aspx?direct=true&db=eric&AN=EJ1095156&site=eds-live.

Watkins, Matthew. "Battered by Harvey, Texas College Students Struggle to Start Class." The Texas Tribune, 30 August 2017. www.texastribune.org/2017/08/30/battered-harvey-texas-college-students-struggle-start-class/.

Watson, George and James Sottile. "Cheating in the Digital Age: Do Students Cheat More in Online Courses?" Online Journal of Distance Learning Administration, vol. 13, no. 1, 2010. www.westga.edu/~distance/ojdla/spring131/watson131.html.

Webb, Michael, Mayka, Liz. "Unconventional Wisdom: A Profile of the Graduates of Early College High School." Jobs for the Future, Mar. 2011, www.jff.org/publications/unconventional-wisdom-profile-graduates-early-college-high-school.

West, James A. and Amanda J. Shoemaker. "The Differences in Syllabi Development for Traditional Classes Compared to Online Courses: A Review of the Literature." The International Journal of Technology, Knowledge, and Society, vol. 8, no. 1, 2012, pp. 116-122. EBSCOhost, ezproxy.mclennan.edu/login?url=http://search.ebscohost.com/login.aspx?direct=true&db=a9h&AN=91544676&site=eds-live.

Westermann, Edward B. "A Half-Flipped Classroom or an Alternative Approach?: Primary Sources and Blended Learning." Educational Research Quarterly, vol. 38, no. 2, Dec. 2014, pp. 43–57.

Western Interstate Commission for Higher Education. The North American Network of Science Labs Online—Expanding Student Access to STEM Fields. 17 March 2015. www.wiche.edu/info/nanslo/NANSLO%20Overview%203-17-2015.pdf.

"What is the Median Usage of People on Your Network Today?" Xfinity. December 2016. www.xfinity.com/support/internet/data-usage-average-network-usage/.

"What Is Project Based Learning (PBL)?" What Is PBL? | Project Based Learning | BIE, Buck Institute for Education, www.bie.org/about/what_pbl.

"What Is UDL?" National Center on Universal Design for Learning. 31 July 2014. www.udlcenter.org/aboutudl/whatisudl.

"What is Universal Design?" Centre for Excellence in Universal Design. universaldesign.ie/What-is-Universal-Design/. Accessed 22 November 2017.

White, S., Olenick, B., and Bray, T. "College students on the autism spectrum: prevalence and associated problems." Autism, 2011, Nov;15(6):683-701.

Whittaker, Alexandra L., Gordon S. Howarth and Kerry A. Lymn. "Evaluation of Facebook to Create an Online Learning Community in an Undergraduate Animal Science Class." Educational Media International, vol. 51, no. 2, 2014, pp. 135-145. EBSCOhost, doi:10.1080/09523987.2014.924664.

Wiedmer, Terry. "Generations Do Differ: Best Practices in Leading Traditionalists, Boomers, and Generations x, y, and z." The Delta Kappa Gamma Bulletin: International Journal for Professional Educators, vol. 82, no. 1, 2015, pp. 51–58.

Willging, Pedro A. and Scott D. Johnson. "Factors That Influence Students' Decision to Dropout of Online Courses." Journal of Asynchronous Learning Networks, vol. 13, no. 3, 2009, pp. 115-127. EBSCOhost, ezproxy.mclennan.edu/login?url=http://search.ebscohost.com/login.aspx?direct=true&db=eric&AN=EJ862360&site=eds-live.

Wieman, Carl E. and Katherine K. Perkins. "A Powerful Tool for Teaching Science." Nature Physics, vol. 2, no. 5, 2006, pp. 290-292. EBSCOhost, doi:10.1038/nphys283.

Williams, Vicki. Online Readiness Assessment. pennstate.qualtrics.com/jfe/form/SV_7QCNUPsyH9f012B?s=246aa3a5c4b64bb386543eab834f8e75. Accessed 25 November 2017.

Wilson, Janell D., Sheila A. Codry and Nina King. "Building Learning Communities with Distance Learning Instruction." TechTrends: Linking Research & Practice to Improve Learning, vol. 48, no. 6, 2004, pp. 20-22. EBSCOhost, ezproxy.mclennan.edu/login?url=http://search.ebscohost.com/login.aspx?direct=true&db=a9h&AN=15835492&site=eds-live.

Wilson, Karen and James H. Korn. "Attention During Lectures: Beyond Ten Minutes." Teaching of Psychology, vol. 34, no. 2, 2007, pp. 85-89. EBSCOhost, ezproxy.mclennan.edu/login?url=http://search.ebscohost.com/login.aspx?direct=true&db=ofm&AN=507971719&site=eds-live.

Wilson, Leslie Owen. "Understanding the New Version of Bloom's Taxonomy." The Second Principle, 2013. www.thesecondprinciple.com/teaching-essentials/beyond-bloom-cognitive-taxonomy-revised/.

Winstead, S. "7 Technical Tips for Creating Video Lectures." elearningbrothers.com, June, 2016. Retrieved June 6, 2017 from the World Wide Web: http://elearningbrothers.com/7-technical-tips-for-creating-video-lectures/.

World Economic Forum. "Human Capital Outlook." http://www3.weforum.org/docs/WEF_ASEAN_HumanCapitalOutlook.pdf. 2016.

Wong, Lily, et al. "A Framework for Investigating Blended Learning Effectiveness." Education Training, vol. 56, no. 2/3, Aug. 2014, pp. 233–251.

Wu, Ruohan and Xueyu Cheng. "Grades Difference Before and After Using an Online Interactive Homework System - A Case Study in Teaching Economics at Alabama State University." Journal of Economics and Economic Education Research, vol. 16, no. 3, 2015, pp. 253-263. EBSCOhost, ezproxy.mclennan.edu/login?url=http://search.ebscohost.com/login.aspx?direct=true&db=edsgsb&AN=edsgcl.459170475&site=eds-live.

Zepke, Nick, and Linda Leach. "Improving Student Engagement: Ten Proposals for Action." Active Learning in Higher Education, vol. 11, no. 3, 2010, pp. 167–177.

Zhang, Jinsong and Richard T. Walls. "Instructors' Self-Perceived Pedagogical Principle Implementation in the Online Environment." Quarterly Review of Distance Education, vol. 7, no. 4, Winter 2006, pp. 413-450.

Index

E

F

G

Q

R

S

If you found this book helpful, you'll want to check out these other Part-Time Press titles:

The Power of Blended Learning in the Sciences

Take your science courses to the next level....

• Design science courses that are fun to teach.

• Improve student learning outcomes.

• Spend less time lecturing and more time teaching.

• Learn to use blending to teach any type of science course or lab.

The Power of Blended Learning in the Sciences is a soup to nuts guide to everything you need to know about how to design courses in this format. The guiding theme of the book is that blended learning is not just another pedagogical fad, but rather an excellent framework for improving your teaching practice. While targeted for those who teach in the sciences, instructors in all disciplines will benefit from the accessible advice, well-structured format, and engaging writing. *The Power of Blended Learning in the Sciences* is available in paperback for $20.00.

New! Blended Learning & Flipped Classrooms: A Comprehensive Guide

Wish your students....

• Took responsibility for their learning?

• Completed coursework and actively participated in classroom discussions?

• Completed assigned work on time?

• Turned in assignments that followed directions/rubrics?

Flipped classrooms combined with blended learning strategies and techniques allow teaching faculty to combine their own creativity with technological tools that can make all of these "wishes" (and more) come true. Students in flipped and blended courses are more engaged, prepared and excited about the course materials you are eager to teach. Authors Patricia Adams and Happy Gingras—award-winning faculty members—have been teaching flipped and blended college courses for over a decade and in this book they take readers step-by-step through the process of flipping and blending a course. *Blended Learning & Flipped Classrooms* is available in paperback for $20.00.

Visit Part-TimePress.com